Eyes On
WINNING WAYS

Eyes On
WINNING WAYS

A Roadmap to Master Your Personal and Professional Life

Joe Guella

Eyes On WINNING WAYS

A Roadmap to Master Your Personal & Professional Life

Published in the United States of America by
Eyes On Communications LLC
120 E. Main St
Suite 317
Ramsey, NJ 07446
Orders: www.eyesoncommunications.com

Copyright © 2011 by Joe Guella

All rights reserved. No part of this book may be reproduced, stored in a retrieval system, or transmitted in any form or by any means, electronic or mechanical, including photocopying, recording or by any information storage and retrieval system, without prior written permission from the author, except for the inclusion of brief quotations in a review.

First Edition, 2011
Library of Congress Control Number: 2011936289

Publisher's Cataloging-in-Publication data
Guella, Joe
Eyes On WINNING WAYS: A Roadmap to Master Your Personal & Professional Life
Eyes On Communications LLC, Publisher
226 p. 23 cm.
Includes bibliographical references and index
ISBN-13: 978-0-9839100-0-8

1. Self-actualization (Psychology).   2. Success - Psychological aspects.   3. Career changes.   4. Goal.   5. Character.   I. Title.
158.1   2011936289

In Memory of my Father and Mother who taught me about life, those things to acknowledge, accept, or change. Although they were deaf, they moved through life accepting their situation, yet not allowing the world to place unnecessary limits on them.

You can live
life your way!

Table of Contents

PREFACE .... **i**
   YOU CAN TRANSFORM YOUR LIFE .... *II*
   BACKGROUND .... *III*
   BOOK FORMAT .... *VI*

ACKNOWLEDGEMENTS .... **vii**

INTRODUCTION **19**
   CHANGE YOUR LIFE *20*
   GETTING STARTED - THE PATH TO SUCCESS *27*

SELF-INITIATION **33**
   BREAK THE PATTERN *33*
   NEEDS, WANTS, AND DESIRES *35*
   MOTIVATION *36*
   ESTEEM *38*
   CHOICES *39*
   CONTROL *40*
   MAKE IT REAL *42*

STEP 1 *SELF-AWARENESS (WHO AM I?)* ... 49
   GETTING TO KNOW YOURSELF *50*
   MASLOW'S NEEDS HIERARCHY *53*
   PERSONAL INVENTORY *56*
   PERSONALITY TYPES *58*
   ASSESSMENT TESTS *58*
   YOUR CURRENT REALITY *66*
   WOTS UP ANALYSIS *67*
   YOUR PERSONAL INVENTORY *71*

STEP 2 GUIDING PRINCIPLES (MY BELIEFS) 93

    DEFINITIONS 94
    GUIDING PRINCIPLES..95
    EXAMPLE OF GUIDING PRINCIPLES...................................104
    YOUR PERSONAL CODE OF CONDUCT..............................109

STEP 3 SELF-ASSURED (CREATE YOUR COMPELLING FUTURE) 111

    STRATEGIZE FOR CHANGE..112
    TRAINING THE SUBCONSCIOUS MIND 112
    PROGRAM YOUR SUCCESS 113
    POSITIVE SENSORY VISUALIZATION 117
    AFFIRMATIONS..119

STEP 4 VISION & MISSION (YOUR ASPIRATIONS & PURPOSE) 125

    YOUR MAJOR DEFINITE PURPOSE.....................................126
    CREATE YOUR PERSONAL VISION......................................127
    PERSONAL MISSION STATEMENT 132
    ROLES 138
    CREATE YOUR MIND MAP 140

STEP 5 GOAL SETTING (DEVELOP THE PATH) 147

    GOALS 148
    SETTING GOALS EFFECTIVELY 150
    CATEGORIES OF IMPORTANCE 152
    OTHER FACTORS 154
    GOAL ACHIEVEMENT...161

STEP 6 LIFE MANAGEMENT (PLAN THE WORK AND WORK THE PLAN) 163

    PLAN THE WORK & WORK THE PLAN 164
    DECISION MAKING & RISK TAKING (DECISION IS A RISK ROOTED IN COURAGE) 176
    SUPPORT TEAMS (HELP IS THERE FOR YOU)....................179

PERSERVERANCE (THE TOUGH GETS GOING WHEN THE GOING GETS TOUGH).. *184*
INTEGRATION (BRINGING IT ALL TOGETHER) *192*

STEP 7 *SELF-RENEWAL (RECHARGE YOUR ENERGY SOURCE)*... *199*

SPIRITUAL.. *203*
INTELLECTUAL... *204*
PSYCHOLOGICAL/SOCIAL *205*
PHYSICAL... *206*

EPILOGUE – FIT FOR LIFE 209
GLOSSARY.. 211
BIBLIOGRAPHY 215
INDEX... 221

LIST of ACTION ITEMS

See last paragraph on page 30 for more information about ACTION ITEMS and their use.

#	CHAPTER	PAGE	TOPIC
1	Self-Initiation	44	Set up methodology to document your efforts & actions. Create your "Desires" list.
2	Self-Assessment	69	Perform a Self-Assessment.
3	Guiding Principles	101	Determine & document your Guiding Principles.
4	Guiding Principles	109	Align your performance (guiding principles & actions).
5	Self-Assurance	119	Visualization Techniques.
6	Self-Assurance	121	Positive Affirmations.
7	Vision & Mission	130	Writing your vision statement.
8	Vision & Mission	134	Writing your mission statement.
9	Vision & Mission	139	Document your roles.
10	Vision & Mission	143	Draw a mind map.
11	Goal Setting	156	List your goals.
12	Goal Setting	159	Goal prioritization.
13	Life Management	166	Creating To-Do lists.
14	Life Management	171	Schedule important activities.
15	Life Management	173	Develop plan to fulfill your goals.
16	Life Management	179	Practice decision making.
17	Life Management	184	Role models & team support.
18	Life Management	195	Create a Mind Map.
19	Self-Renewal	197	Establish a schedule of periodic reviews of your plan.
20	Self-Renewal	204	Schedule spiritual alignment time.
21	Self-Renewal	205	Schedule Reading time for intellectual stimulation.
22	Self-Renewal	205	Schedule Family time.
23	Self-Renewal	207	Schedule a Health Check.

PREFACE

> *"When you are inspired by some great purpose, some extraordinary project, all your thoughts break their bonds: Your mind transcends limitations, your consciousness expands in every direction, and you find yourself in a new, great, and wonderful world. Dormant forces, faculties, and talents become alive, and you discover yourself to be greater person by far than you ever dreamed yourself to be."* - Patanjali, compiler of Yoga Sutras, 2nd century B.C.

Most of us would like to transform ourselves. We desire to accomplish more in life and be effective in whatever we do. In addition, we want to be self-reliant whatever our current situation happens to be. This book is for those of us who want and expect more from life. We want to be active participants in living our lives and feel useful towards societal activities.

While anyone can find this book useful and not intending to limit the audience, a few key groups are identified as follows:

    a) Unemployed or under-employed and looking for

another position or a recent college graduate who is trying to decide what to do now that school is over. Everyone recognizes it is a very competitive job market and we need every bit of help we can get.

b) Moms who are desirous of re-entering the job market and are seeking guidance as to what to do now in their life. Their knowledge and experience may be dated and their self-confidence either weakened or destroyed.

c) Drifters going through life doing what is expected of them rather than doing what they want. They may have not taken the time to think through what it is that they want yet feel that something is missing.

YOU CAN TRANSFORM YOUR LIFE

Whatever the circumstances that brought you here, this book provides a process that will focus your aspirations and purpose, and transform your life. You will perform a self-assessment and identify your guiding principles, vision, and mission. Applying some additional techniques, you will identify where you want to be and establish goals to get you there. This process details a series of steps when applied will provide a solid foundation for you to transform your life and become a winner.

The process is a methodology to change your life. By identifying your guiding principles, vision, and mission, you will have started on the path to success and self-fulfillment. You will discover how to:

- ➢ Take command of your life and change your personal circumstances.
- ➢ Create your compelling future while converting your dreams into reality.
- ➢ Broaden your awareness of yourself, your potential, and your positive qualities.
- ➢ Identify and capitalize on your strengths and increase

your self-confidence and self-esteem.
- ➢ End self-defeating behaviors and utilize the abilities you have to create positive change.
- ➢ Create a future of your own when you develop your vision, mission, and goals.
- ➢ Increase personal productivity by way of a daily planning and action process.
- ➢ Become fully engaged in life and face every day with expectation and excitement.
- ➢ Become a person of action who lives life your way.

BACKGROUND

Over the last twenty years, our society has witnessed dramatic changes that have had a greater impact upon our lives than the last few centuries has had. Not only have the changes had an impact in the United States but globally. The world has become an even more complex place in which we live our lives. Mechanization, modernization, and computerization plus instantaneous communications have created dramatic changes to the factory, office, and home. Even the social environment has changed radically by the use of MySpace, Facebook, LinkedIn, Twitter, etc.

Furthermore, people think about work and career environments very differently than in the past. Previously, people had one path in life and that was all there was for them. Today, it is very likely a person will change careers multiple times because either change is forced upon them or they want or need the change. Older people are experiencing dissatisfaction with their chosen careers, younger people are confused about their future, and everyone is trying to find the right path to take.

In order to accomplish positive change in our lives, we need to be able to assess and understand our current situation and know where, what, and why we see a new or different future for ourselves.

As you start this book, you may wonder, "Why is Joe writing this book?" and possibly "What expertise does he have?" My many years of experience in business involved with and managing people from around the world and my personal experiences caused me to realize that the key part of being a good manager was to teach, train, and encourage people how to plan and accomplish things in their life. I was able to help them achieve success in both their business and their personal lives. I realized that I was instrumental and am good at helping people to acknowledge and achieve their potential.

There have been numerous self-improvement books written by reputable, well-known authors, who have worked through techniques, proposed systematic or other approaches espousing their philosophy on how to become a winner by transforming your life and career. It is important to decipher which are fads and which present useful and applicable information. The bibliography at the back of this book includes several useful references.

The first good self-help book I read to transform oneself was Psycho-Cybernetics, first published in 1960. In it, Dr. Maxwell Maltz put forth the principle that self-image is the key to all human behavior. He compared the sub-conscious to the homing system in a torpedo. Once you set the target, the self-adjusting mechanism continuously monitors feedback signals from the target and uses that information to adjust the course constantly guiding the torpedo toward the target.

In order to describe the human process of accomplishment, Dr. Maltz created the term Psycho-Cybernetics, which means, "steering your mind to a productive goal." The sub-conscious mind behaves in much the same way as the torpedo. Once you set your goal and program it properly, your subconscious constantly monitors the feedback about your goal. If you are off course towards accomplishing your goal, your mind makes adjustments so you will reach your goal. If you take the necessary time preparing your mind and believe in what you are trying to achieve, you will have programmed your subconscious mind and it will guide you towards your goal.

You can find examples from all aspects of life, such as in athletics, business, medicine, politics, etc., of people who have done this. It is even very likely you personally know people who have accomplished the goals in their lives. They set their goal, utilized a positive attitude coupled with a plan and a burning desire to accomplish a specific goal. They added the dedication and effort required to accomplish great achievements.

After doing significant research, reading and listening to what the guru's proposed, organizing their methods, and observing successful people, I developed a seven-step process. This process is a distillation of those best practices that will make a difference for you. My effort has resulted in a system that is simple and will work for anyone who will follow the system and perform the steps of the process. In my managerial capacity, I coached people on applying the steps and it resulted in a positive impact on their lives.

Many of us expect quick answers even before we know exactly what it is we want. We expect quick results through mini-learning. We live with expectations of quick and simple answers to any questions about any topic; even our news and media are comprised of short bits of information called "sound-bites." Just think about that as it applies to your life and your expectations. I believe we all know that anything worth accomplishing takes focused and planned efforts.

This book will teach you powerful steps necessary to achieve personal success. It will help you to become all that you want to be. It takes focus and planned effort. Achievement is not automatic, however it is possible if you:

- accept and *believe* in the principles that you will learn, and
- *dedicate* the required *time* and *effort* necessary to facilitate those newly learned principles.

Winners achieve their dreams when they apply the known principles in a systematic way. As a person who has years of experience as a manager and who has been very effective counseling and developing people, I can help you. The seven steps will guide you through the process, which is SIMPLE, but it will not be *EASY!* It does require you to sustain the motivation to exert *EFFORT* continuously and the seven-step system will become a change in your whole approach to life.

> *"The only thing that stands between a man and what he wants from life is often merely the will to try it and the faith to believe that it is possible."* - **David Viscott**

BOOK FORMAT

The Introduction presents a summary of the seven-step process. The chapters contain information to read and study as well as additional information and forms to document your efforts. They also contain one or more "ACTION ITEMS" to accomplish.

In addition, you will need to create a document, whether it be hard copy or electronic, to record your progress. As you go through the Steps of the program, it will be helpful to have one place to document your answers to the various questions and ACTION ITEMS. You will see both the big picture evolving as well as the items, such as your daily To-Do lists.

Joe Guella
Chester, NJ
September 2011

ACKNOWLEDGEMENTS

My grateful appreciation goes to all the people who helped to make this book possible. Many people worked with and for me over the years and provided the basis and experience to make this book possible. I have learned so much from them.

Long before I thought about this book, my parents, through their example, taught me about values, service to others, and enjoyment of life and family. Additionally, I want to thank my wife for her love, support, and patience over the years.

My daughter Jodi Guella and my sister Trudy Guella provided feedback on the manuscript and insights for the overall project.

Penny Maroules provided much needed critical editing of the manuscript. Any remaining errors are my responsibility. Athena Maroules provided initial graphical design help.

Recognition for the efforts put forth by the people from the Professional Services Group (PSG) of Morris County, New Jersey, starting with Elena Collins who provided encouragement and support. Also, the team of 15 [Barbara Such, Barry Goldfarb, Elaine Green, Frank Magdits, Gail Avery, Geraldine Cataudella, Joselyn Conti, Lucia Lee, Mark Muschko, Maureen Fanning, Michael McSharry, Paul Sicardo, Sam Sandus, Sandra Liese, and Sunny Shahinian] who endured my ramblings and provided valuable input.

Grateful acknowledgement is offered for the use of the

following material:

The "Your Personal Inventory" questionnaire, which is being used with modifications, originally developed by Michael E. Angier, Copyright 2000 Success Networks International, Inc., Version 1.2 02/2001 from URL www.SuccessNet.org.

Girl Scouts of the United States of America for permission to reprint the Girl Scout Promise and Girl Scout Law.

BrainyQuote.com, Xplore Inc., for providing access to the David Viscott quotes on November 2, 2010 at the following sites: http://www.brainyquote.com/quotes/quotes/d/davidvisco381240.html, and http://www.brainyquote.com/quotes/quotes/d/davidvisco381241.html.

While I have used concepts introduced by many different sources including the bible, I particularly would like to commend the following sources:

a) Concepts introduced in Psycho-Cybernetics by Dr. Maxwell Maltz and Psycho-Cybernetics 2000 by Bobbe Sommer and Maxwell Maltz Foundation.

b) Concepts introduced by Stephen Covey in his books, especially The Seven Habits of Highly Effective People and First Things First.

c) Concepts introduced by Anthony Robbins in his books Unlimited Power and Awaken the Giant Within.

Disclaimer: "Eyes On Winning Ways: A Roadmap to Master Your Personal and Professional Life" is not an official publication of Girl Scouts of the United States of America. This product is not endorsed nor sponsored by Girl Scouts of the United States of America.

INTRODUCTION

> *"To be what we are, and to become what we are capable of becoming, is the only end of life."* - Robert Louis Stevenson, Of Men and Books, 1882

Each one of us begins at a different point based on experience and varying stages of desire to make changes in his or her life. Achieving change is impossible if all we do is complain about our current situation and only dream of what we would like our situation to become. The necessary questions we must ask ourselves are:

- How motivated am I to make changes in my life?
- How badly do I want to achieve my full potential?
- What are my guiding principles or core beliefs?
- What are my goals?
- Do I have a written list of goals to remind me?
- Do I have a plan to accomplish my goals?
- How will I know when and how well I have achieved them?

Most of us desire change but we do not have answers to those key questions nor do we have a systematic method of achieving them. We have not taken the time to look deeply inside ourselves. Knowing and understanding who we are and what we want to become is the starting point. Identifying and understanding what our Guiding Principles and goals are will be the basis for establishing a plan of action that will ultimately give us more control over our lives. Follow through and accomplishment of our goals will both bring change & satisfaction, thus, enabling us to transform our lives into what we want it to be.

CHANGE YOUR LIFE

The fact that you are reading this book generally indicates that you are not satisfied with what is happening in your life and you want to make changes, but have not yet been successful. You may want to make changes but may not know how or you do not believe in your ability to make the necessary changes.

All of us have dreams. We dream of a "better" life, however, we have not defined "better". We see ourselves doing things that we are not capable of doing currently, whether it be about our career, personal life, societal works, sense of adventure, or anything else. We dream and see ourselves having more, whether it is accomplishments, family, friends, and/or success. We are *winners!* Dreaming about a different future is a good beginning; however, the purpose of this book is to help you to go further and achieve your greatest dream.

- Do you desire ANSWERS or CHANGES:
    - for career moves?
    - to your personal circumstances?
    - for your relationships?
    - to where you want to be in five years?
    - to help achieve your dreams?
- Do you want to CONVERT your dreams into reality?
- Are you looking for:
    - an effective method to IGNITE your passions?
    - a way to OPEN your mind?
    - an EXPOSURE to new ideas & perspectives?
    - a methodology on how to DEVELOP yourself?

- Do you want to be FULLY ENGAGED in life, facing every day with expectation and excitement?
- Are you ready to TAKE COMMAND of your life?

You will become a winner if you believe!

The first item you must learn, know, and believe in is *YOU* and the power of your mind. You must develop the confidence in your ability to do what is required. For many people, this will require a paradigm shift; that is, a revolutionary transformation, or drastic change in your basic approach to life.

Therefore, a paradigm shift will come when you learn, understand, & believe the mind is great, powerful, and will accomplish whatsoever you will tell it is possible. You are in control if you allow yourself to believe in your abilities. Although we have learned so much about the human mind and body, we are only scratching the surface. We are utilizing only a tiny fraction of our brains potential.

You will learn to create the person you will become. As you proceed through this book, you will need an open and absorbent mind to assimilate all kinds of information. Both the process presented and your inner voice will guide your efforts. However, your development can only succeed by making use of your own mental powers.

As we learn, we find new ways to apply that knowledge. The human mind is capable of "creating a reality" through our subconscious. If our subconscious believes in a *"reality"* then it is real to us. We will discuss two ways that you can utilize the creative imagination of your subconscious mind. The first is to have the imagination to create the situation and the strength to bring it out for the world to see.

There are concepts based on ancient philosophies. For example, in the "Star Wars" movies created by George Lucas, the concept of utilizing *"The Force"* to help you battle and conquer evil demonstrates the ability of utilizing the human psyche to produce unbelievable results.

In the first movie of the trilogy, called "Star Wars," Obi-Wan Kenobi taught Luke Skywalker about *The Force*. He told Luke
"A Jedi can feel The Force flowing through him."

Luke asked
"You mean it controls your actions?"

Obi-Wan Kenobi explains
"Partially, but it also obeys your commands."

In the second movie, Yoda, a Jedi master, taught Luke the proper techniques so that Luke could utilize *The Force*. Yoda explained to Luke
"You must unlearn what you have learned."

At another point Luke told Yoda
"I don't believe it."

At which Yoda responded
"That is why you fail."

Eventually Luke learns to believe and how to utilize *The Force* in a positive manner. Of course, he had to practice, practice, and practice to make it all possible.

Yes, that was fiction but the concept is real. Someday, people will harness the power of *The Force*. Meanwhile, we can take steps towards utilizing the power of our subconscious mind to create a new reality for ourselves. The ability and power is there for you to harness but as Yoda told Luke, you must believe and practice to be able to harness the power within you.

The best example of the power of the mind to conceive concepts that have subsequently become reality is in the writings of Jules Verne (1828-1905). The "Father of Science Fiction" wrote about underwater, air, and space travel long before practical submarines and aircraft, especially spaceships were invented. Most of the concepts that Jules Verne presented over one hundred years ago in his stories and believed to be science fiction have become reality. He conceived stories about submarines and exploration of the undersea world, or rockets and exploration of the moon long before anyone thought it would be feasible.

Other people, who believed in the creative concepts presented by Jules Verne, were able to develop those ideas and make them into realities. We now have both submarines and rockets; and we have put people on the moon. These accomplishments demonstrate one facet of the power of the mind to first conceive and then to create.

The second way to utilize the power of your mind is to use your imagination to set a goal, but this time, visualize and believe in your ability to create the outcome. Think of your greatest heroes and/or heroines. Whom do you admire? Is that person an athlete, movie star, writer, scientist, or politician? Is it a great figure from history, from your family, or a current person? It will help to focus on their background, where they came from, and what they accomplished. How do you think they achieved whatever it was that they achieved? As you look deeper into their situation, you will undoubtedly find that they had a dream or an outcome they visualized and believed would come true. In addition to the dream, they had a well-executed plan. Success did not come quickly but rather slowly over time.

Let us look at an example of a goal developed with a positive attitude and the action and dedication necessary to achieve the desired outcome. It was December 24th and for some, it was Christmas Eve, which was a time of religious celebration. A group, of dirty and disheveled men, was outdoors and feeling the effects of the unusually cold weather. They huddled together as they got into a boat to cross the Delaware River from Pennsylvania to New Jersey. One man stood alone peering into the night, almost impervious to the cold. This was to be an important boat ride. The year was 1776 and the man standing was George Washington leading his Continental Army in two bold attacks on the British, first in Trenton and then on to Princeton, on Christmas morning.

Here was a group of rag-tag men without any real experience as soldiers. They were now the Continental Army, with little in the way of provisions, fighting a war against well trained and provisioned, smartly uniformed, and combat experienced regular Army professionals. The American Revolution was all but lost, however the men were following their leader, their commander-in-chief, who had a vision and a plan. The surprise attack and the sheer will of the Americans resulted in two very important victories, the first in Trenton and then in Princeton.

These two victories proved to be very important to the Continental Army as they confiscated much needed ammunition, food and other supplies from their enemy. Furthermore, the victories and supplies gave the soldiers courage, hope, and newfound confidence that helped them survive the brutal winter.

Most Americans are familiar with the painting of "Washington Crossing the Delaware." What made George Washington attempt this military action? George Washington saw an opportunity, believed in his men and their abilities, and the men believed in their leader. It was due to George Washington having a clear vision, beliefs, and a well-executed plan that made this raid successful and this action became the turning point of the American Revolution. Much was yet to come but the war was won on the vision, plan, and action taken that night.

Two hundred plus years later, we have become a society reacting to 10-second sound bites. We get, expect, and receive short and quick answers to the most complex issues we live with. We have come to expect instant answers, and thus gratification, with minimal effort. The 10-second sound bites would have undermined George Washington and his troop's efforts. Imagine what would have happened during the

Revolutionary War if the reporting and subsequent actions were evaluated based on today's 10-second sound bite standards.

When you attempt to make personal changes, it is your self-image, which the subconscious mind sees and believes in, that determines your accomplishments; however, you need to work somewhat within your physical limitations. For example, someone who is 5' 5" tall is not going to become the center for a professional basketball team but may excel in another athletic endeavor. You must be honest with yourself, be self-confident, be determined, and be ready and able to accomplish many great undertakings.

Look at some of the examples of winners that you can see had an impact on major areas of our lives. Study the accomplishments of people such as Andrew Carnegie in steel, Henry Ford in automobiles, Thomas Edison in electricity, the Wright brothers in aviation, Alexander Graham Bell in telephony, Bill Gates, Steve Jobs, or Michael Dell in computers, Ray Kroc (McDonald's) or Dave Thomas (Wendy's) in fast food, and Donald Trump or Richard Branson in modern business. These people had both the vision and drive to create a new reality. Their work created a new world that has taken society into areas that it had never been before. Any setbacks they had did not deter them from the direction they wanted to travel. They may have had to change course a bit but they continued towards their destination. More dramatic changes have occurred in the last 100 years than had cumulatively occurred in the previous 2000 years.

Many of us can relate to someone in the sports arena. If that is your case, you can study the achievements of athletes in your favorite sport, such as Tiger Woods in golf, Michael Jordan in basketball, Venus and Serena Williams in tennis, etc. Choose the sport you follow and look at its star player. Those people had to believe in themselves and work at accomplishing their goals within their respective sport. Investigate how much time they had to spend practicing to become super in their field of endeavor. Even the so-called "natural" athletes had to work at becoming the super-star.

Another perspective is to look at the universe around us. The Bible tells us God created the universe over seven periods of creation. Although the translation is that each period is a "day", the Hebrew word is "Yom" which means a defined period. You can interpret the period to be however long you think is appropriate. Scientists estimate that the beginning occurred some billions of years ago. The important thing is to recognize that the universe took time to evolve into what we know and see today. Following the Bible, Genesis 1.1 states, "In the beginning God created the universe; the earth was formless and desolate..." Let us follow what happened:

- Day 1 - God commanded, "Let there be light" and with that, God made light to separate from darkness. Day and night passed and it was the first day.
- Day 2 - Then God commanded, "Let there be a dome to divide the water and to keep it in two separate places...He named the dome "Sky." Evening passed and morning came – that was the second day.
- Day 3 - God created Earth and Sea and commanded, "Let the earth produce all kinds of plants..."
- Day 4 - With clear skies, the sun, moon, and stars were visible and they served as signs to mark days, months, seasons, and years.
- Day 5 - God created birds and sea creatures during the next day.
- Day 6 - God created vast numbers of land animals and MAN.
- Day 7 - When the whole universe was completed, God had finished His work and on this day, He rested.

God created the universe following a logical process and a series of steps over time. We want to "create" a new person and our expectation is to do it in a short period, such as a "day." The reality is that it took us years to get to this point in our lives; it will take some time to enact the change we desire.

GETTING STARTED - THE PATH TO SUCCESS

This is a comprehensive systems approach to understand our patterns of behavior, the underlying reasons, and the methodology to effect changes and solve problems. It is based on years of personal experience of doing and seeing others work the process.

This approach addresses the need for key steps that are synergistic to create a total process. One must initially take these steps as a series that delivers you to your destination. Some people favor the use of their right brain while others favor the left-brain. Some people are visual and creative while others are logical and analytical. I am going to teach you a process that uses both sides of your brain. You are going to make maximum use of the gifts you have. If you believe in the process and work it, you will become a winner.

People who have great accomplishments utilize the path to success by following these seven steps in a synergistic process. The steps are:

1. *Self-Awareness* – It is critical to conduct a situation audit of your personal Strengths & Weaknesses and environmental Opportunities & Threats/Constraints. This will enable you to know and understand your abilities, emotions, and feelings that may have affected your performance in the past. This provides a baseline or starting point for the journey.

2. *Guiding Principles* – Having and following a set of clearly defined values and principles provides the basis of what guides you and a crucial insight to how you approach life. Knowing the relative importance of each Guiding Principle will dictate how you react to specific situations.

3. ***Self-Assured*** - Stimulate your mind to conceive new ideas and create plans. Use positive sensory visualization and affirmations to help set your expectations, develop your self-confidence, believe in what you can achieve, and enjoy what you do.

4. ***Vision & Mission*** – This effort utilizes the concepts of Positive Mental Attitude (PMA) and Psycho-Cybernetics to do away with aimlessness and create a strong well-defined purpose. Use those tools to create your vision and mission for your future. Use feature rich visions of what you want to achieve in each of the roles you have in life. "See" the result via your Mind Map.

5. ***Goal Setting*** – Use your vision, mission, and purpose to develop some well-conceived goals. Examine the areas of your life that need to be addressed to fulfill your dreams. Once goals are set, the process moves to the next step of identification and evaluation of strategies to achieve them.

6. ***Life Management*** – Manage your behavior and actions; develop clear and actionable plans to create a compelling future.

    a. ***Decision Making & Risk Taking*** - Focus your attention to concentrate your efforts, know how and when to acquire essential skills, learn how to separate important facts from simply information, make decisions, and take calculated risks necessary to move forward with your plan.

    b. ***Support Teams*** - Seek out positive role models for inspiration and learning, coordinate your effort with others, establish an alliance, and use cooperation to utilize the team to accomplish your goals.

c. *Perseverance* - Have patience to achieve your goal, do not give up when it gets tough to accomplish, learn the difference between failure and temporary defeat and make stepping-stones out of your mistakes and failures.

d. *Integration* – Bring it all together and formulate specific plans to implement the goals.

7. *Self-Renewal* – Make time to re-charge your energy source, maintain good health, and practice your faith.

The following diagram depicts the seven steps:

The step identified as Self-Renewal is at the center of the

diagram and is connected to each of the other steps. While there is a logical flow from step to step, this process is a feedback system that may require you to jump steps. Take notice that all the connecting lines have arrows pointing at each end. They depict that your actions working the process may require going to a different step or taking a step back before proceeding forward. Ideally, the diagram would show a connecting line from each step to all the other steps.

Initially, you will work Steps 1 to 5 in a sequential manner.

In Step 1, you will conduct a situation audit of your personal *S*trengths & *W*eaknesses and environmental *O*pportunities & *T*hreats/Constraints. Known as a *SWOT* analysis, I like to rearrange the letters and say that this type of analysis tells us *WOTS* up. You should be as honest and thorough as possible when you conduct this self-analysis.

Step 2 examines your belief system.

Step 3 helps you to develop your ability to create your future.

Step 4 assists you to clarify your aspirations and life purpose.

Step 5 works on the identification and evaluation of goals (strategies) to achieve them. Each goal will involve sub-goals or To-Do lists.

Step 6 brings everything together into a comprehensive effort. It is here where you will formulate specific plans to implement your goals.

Step 7 is the hub of the wheel to keep us rolling with our efforts. You can move into this step at any time. We must keep ourselves energized to be able to continue to roll on and to be able to bounce back from setbacks. Keep your energy high and you will find yourself rolling along crossing ruts and bumps with ease.

As you go through this book, think of it as a seminar or course that you are taking. You should not only read the book, but also, it must be *experienced* in order to get the most from it. There are exercises entitled "ACTION ITEMS" for you to work at and ideas to contemplate. The more time and effort you put into these ACTION ITEMS will enable you to reap the benefits of achieving your goals.

This book provides you with the fundamental information that you will need to accomplish each step; however, know that there are volumes written on the intricate details of each topic within the steps. As and when you feel the need for additional information, you can research and read other materials. The bibliography can serve as a starting point. You will get from the effort in proportion to the effort you put into it. The process works if you work the process diligently.

Practice the techniques regularly and do not become discouraged if the results do not go your way immediately. You have habits that have taken years to learn, that now must be unlearned and replaced with new habits. This effort takes time and you will be continuously learning along the way. If you stay with it, you will make the needed changes to become the *WINNER* you want to become.

"No one is ready for a thing until he believes he can acquire it." - **Napoleon Hill**

SELF-INITIATION

> *"If you always do what you've always done, you'll always get what you've always gotten. If you want something different, you have got to do something different."* — Anonymous

The self-initiation process enables us to understand our current circumstances and we can use those circumstances as raw material to transform or create the situations that we want. Principles and values guide proactive choices. Principles are the rules by which we live our life. Values are the things that we hold to be important. Let us first discuss some of our drivers.

BREAK THE PATTERN

Everyone has their own pattern as to the way they observe and react to situations. Before you can transform your life, you need to break the old ways you look at everything around you. So much of what we see and react to emotionally is a function of our perception at that time. When you change your mindset, it will change what you see and do. Look at the following exercises to see examples of differing mindsets.

A) What is it that a rabbit does when it jumps forward? HOP
What does a person use to wipe the floor? MOP
What is another name for a police officer? COP
What do you do at a mall? SHOP
What do you do immediately when you come to a green light?

B) Which way is the cube facing?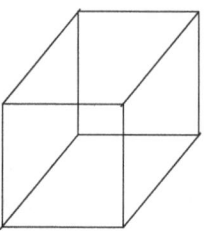

C) Is she a young woman or an old woman? It is from an 1888 German postcard.

Let us look at some answers:

    A) You must "go." If you said, "stop" you are wrong. You were set-up by the pattern of answers to the set of questions.

B) Which way did you see the cube?

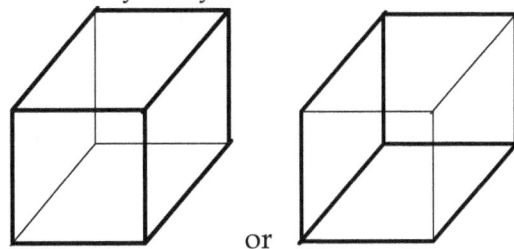

C) Did you see the young woman's profile, her earring, and necklace or did you see the old woman with the large nose?

Conditioning is very easy and we are susceptible to it. If we get into the habit of responding in one way, our quick reaction to similar situations will be similar and possibly incorrect. We must learn how to break habitual patterns and be open to developing new and positive patterns. This requires us to expend continued effort to be alert to unwanted habits and change them into something desirable.

NEEDS, WANTS, AND DESIRES

In order for a person to begin to move away from their current situation towards something they desire, they must know and understand their desires. The road to becoming properly motivated to enact change in ones' life begins with fulfilling *"needs."* Then one will progress to their *"wants"* and finally they will address their *"desires."* My definitions are as follows:

Needs
These are those basic things that we must have. They are things that we require and are a necessity for our survival. In Step 1, we will discuss the hierarchy of needs as put forth by Abraham Maslow.

Wants

We would get these things immediately if there were no restrictions, i.e. no effort is required, no commitment, etc. but we can live without. Many of us stay at this level because it does not require any effort. We simply look around and say I want to have that. Wants without an action plan to make them real are only wishes and remain a want.

Desires

When a want becomes so intense and powerful to drive us to act, it becomes a desire. Desires energize us and push us to reach our goals and fulfill our dreams. We will achieve our desires when we learn to use positive affirmations to convince our subconscious of our abilities. Our passion provides the passion to take the steps to create the environment to support our dreams and transform them into reality.

We must become motivated to make the necessary changes. The motivation supported by a positive self-esteem and positive affirmations takes control of our life and enables us to achieve our desired outcome. The focus must be on developing the mental fortitude to overcome our fears and allow us to achieve our desires.

MOTIVATION

For us to accomplish that which we desire, we must be intensely motivated to achieve the benefits that we want to enjoy. The greater the motivation a person has, the greater the success. Highly motivated people are more productive, achieve more, have better relationships, and are happier than less motivated people are.

We must have a burning craving to accomplish our desired changes, and we must want it badly enough to overcome the current inertia that keeps us on the same track, doing the same things, the same way. No one is going to give it to us, we must have motivation of our own, that is, we have to push ourselves. As we go through these affirmations, the intensity increases until it becomes so strong that we must act. Then, we can take the steps to make our desired changes a reality.

We are responsible and value-driven when we take responsibility for our actions and consciously choose to speak proactively about them. Every day we make choices that affect our behavior and our lives. Motivation enables us to change our language into positive statements and causes us to be proactive. For example, rather than say, "I can't go with you; because I <u>have</u> to work on my project," which implies there is no choice, we can say "I'm not going to go because I <u>prefer</u> to work on the project." The more we develop our ability to choose our responses, the greater freedom we have and the more proactive we become.

People can be motivated by differing factors; discontent with their current situation, by fear, by their achievement drive and/or everything in between. Thad Green, in his book "motivation management," puts forth the concept that, in order for people to become truly motivated, people must believe in three factors. These three key factors deal with a belief in: themselves, that is, to have the confidence to believe they can accomplish what is needed, the accomplishment will result in the desired outcome, and the outcome will provide the needed satisfaction.

You will learn various techniques that will help you to continue to be motivated, such as having a vision, documenting your guiding principles and mission, setting SMART goals, and working the plan. There is a direct correlation between motivation and success. In order to be a winner, you must keep yourself motivated.

In her book "Get Motivated," Tamara Lowe tells us that people have different motivational factors. She describes what she calls "Motivational DNA", which is made up of a combination of factors, "*Desires*," "*Needs*," and "*Awards*" that are unique to each individual and determine exactly what does and does not motivate us. She identifies two modes for each of three categories (Connection/Production, Stability/Variety, Internal/External), which results in eight different motivational types. Her approach is useful to provide us with insights and abilities to understand the factors that motivate us. Since we are all different, we need to learn what motivates us so we may achieve success in achieving our goals.

ESTEEM

We are what we believe we are. It begins in our childhood. We collect thousands of ideas about ourselves as being good, bad, smart, stupid, etc. As we receive repetitive re-enforcement, it becomes our self-image and thus the internal "truth" of how we think of ourselves. Our subconscious produces situations and circumstances, which are consistent with our inner, deepest beliefs.

Our subconscious will always prove that we are correct. When we have a low image of ourselves, or believe we can not accomplish something, we will produce results in line with those beliefs. When we have accepted those false beliefs, they keep us from being all that we could be. We have the power to control our self-image and believe in the right things. We have the power to change our deepest inner beliefs, which will give us the power to change our entire life. We must first believe in ourselves and visualize our accomplishments. We will address how to change our self-image in Step 3.

However, before we get to Step 3, we must spend time to understand where we are and where we want to be. Before we can accomplish change, we have to develop a realistic, current picture of ourselves and know who we are and where we are. Once we know that information, we can think about the changes we want to make. Our self-esteem should be based on the relationship of our sense of competence and worthiness.

Martin Luther King spoke to a group of students at Barratt Junior High School, Philadelphia on October 1967, encouraging them to develop a plan for their lives. He told the students that they should have a belief in their own self-worth and not to allow anyone make them change that belief. Furthermore and linked with the concept of positive self-worth, Reverend King told them to be determined to achieve excellence in everything they do. With this positive self-esteem and the drive for excellence, anything is possible.

CHOICES

All of us have choices to make in our life. It is your life and you must decide how you want to live it. What do you want to accomplish? Are you willing to expend the time and effort required to learn whatever you need to learn? What are you willing to do to ensure you accomplish your dreams? To make it more than a dream, we must set goals for ourselves but most of us tend to fail to set the goals. Why? Because it's uncomfortable and time consuming for us to start. Effectively, we are *SCARED*:

- *S*ubjugated - want to please others and do what others want us to do rather than choosing to do what we want;
- *C*oncerned – about your ability to create your own destiny and the amount of energy needed, so don't try;
- *A*pathetic - tend to not make the time because of laziness or not wanting the change badly enough;
- *R*isk adverse – fear of failure so if you don't try, you can't fail;
- *E*xhausted – busy and not focused; and/or
- *D*oubtful - don't have the confidence of being able to accomplish change;

Living life requires us to make choices every day. We can look back and even understand why we made specific choices but we cannot change the choice we made at some time in the past. We have made our choices, good or bad, and those choices have brought us to this point in our life.

When we examine ourselves now, we can decide if we are or are not on the trajectory we want/need to be following. We can decide to make a new choice to change the course of our life. When we make the choice to steer towards our new destination, we are choosing to move away from something else. In choosing one option, we should recognize we may have to give up something else, such as that easy and relaxing non-controversial life.

Many of us look back at our lives and at some key points say "My life would be different if I had made different decisions." We can blame:

- our parents,
- someone else,
- our destiny, or
- anything else we deem responsible for our current situation.

Children come into this world without knowing any limitations. While some limitations are taught to protect the child, some of us were told either we were incapable of doing certain things or that we did not deserve things we desired. As we grew up, we developed a sense of being incapable or unworthy. Now we need to learn how to shake off the *SCARED* attributes and begin to make positive choices for ourselves.

Ultimately, we must recognize that we bear the responsibility to shape and change our lives. By taking personal responsibility, we can take control of our lives. We must free ourselves from that past – evaluate & learn from the experience and then let it go. We should evaluate our current circumstances and determine what we need to do to create a new, enhanced future. We need to have an attitude that forgives us for our past decisions that we are unhappy about, and choose new paths to move our lives forward towards our new goals.

CONTROL

We need to learn to evaluate situations and make informed

choices. We can control our choices but not the consequences. Once we believe in and have a deep knowledge of ourselves, we can direct our actions toward achieving our goals. We need to limit the things we will work on at any given time. Too many choices have the potential of diverting our efforts and focus. Once we have learned to control our choices, we can focus our energy and can hone in our effort toward fulfilling our desires.

Each of us struggles with some of the same basic issues. We can be concerned about how to live our lives and follow our guiding principles, vision, and mission. In order to be effective, we must take stock of ourselves, understand our beliefs and convictions, set our goals, choose our path, and control our actions. We need to concentrate our effort and not try to change everything at once. We must stop re-acting to situations but instead have planned actions for choices we may be called upon to make. When we limit our areas of attention, we can exert greater control on our actions.

Once you make the decision about what areas need to be changed, you can focus your attention to your identified wants and desires. Controlled attention and concentration of effort on the choice will allow you to put your mind to work to devise a plan to achieve your goal.

Winners focus on their goals. Controlled attention from their conscious mind is taken over by their subconscious mind is essential to their success. It is necessary to have your goal in front of you daily. An action taken the same way repeatedly until the goal is accomplished creates new habits.

Victor Frankl, an author, psychiatrist, and survivor of the Nazi concentration camps, wrote "... last of the human freedoms – the ability to choose one's attitude in any given set of circumstances, to choose one's own way." In his book "Man's Search for Meaning", he explains how he was able to survive three years of horror, including starvation and torture, by mentally disassociating his mind from his body. He talks about how a person can be responsible to live for something however dismal the circumstances.

Frankl explains that each person is unique and therefore so is their mission in life. Each of us should recognize that we have a mission to fulfill and those who do not know that may wither away under difficult circumstances. He believed that those who survived the Nazi concentration camps had a mission known to them that gave the individual the strength to continue rather than give up and die.

> *"In a word, each man is questioned by life; and he can only answer to life by answering for his own life; to life he can only respond by being responsible."* — **Viktor E. Frankl** from Man's Search for Meaning

With the combination of the motivation, proper self-esteem, and controlled attention to your efforts, you can become the steward of your life. You will understand your driving forces, manage your expectations, choose when and where you will apply your efforts, and have the freedom to enjoy the seasons of your life. You will have power over your movements and be in command of your time.

> *"Thinking is easy, acting is difficult, and to put one's thoughts into action is the most difficult thing in the world."* — **Johann Wolfgang von Goethe** (1749 - 1832)

MAKE IT REAL

Everyone in this world has a dream, that is, a vision of their life that pulls and urges them to move forward. What separates those who realize their dreams from those who don't? At the beginning of this section, I told you that the process to become a winner is simple but may not be easy. Here comes the part about it not being easy. You must develop and pursue the following three points:

1) Develop a clear *focus* and *inner clarity* about what is most important in your life.

2) Create an unwavering and deep *passion*, driven by your subconscious mind that provides a spiritual sense of a greater purpose in your life.

3) Keep a profound *commitment* to what you are doing each day.

Anyone *can* become a winner if they believe in themselves and put in the effort necessary to keep on track. They wake up every day knowing there are great things to be created and deeply believe work is fun and not a chore. Winners form habits to do the things that losers do not like to do. It all starts with a dream – a dream of what they want in their future. The dream is vividly pictured in their mind as a reality until it actually becomes a reality.

You can do it as well. It takes having a vision and a positive attitude towards achievement that will make you successful. Your belief in yourself results in the attitude towards your ability to achieve your potential. However, your vision and positive attitude are not sufficient. You must also develop a burning desire and resoluteness to accomplish your goals. The world is filled with an abundance of opportunity that you must be ready to convert into your opportunity. Remember, anything worthwhile, requires planning, hard work, and continuous effort. This book will present techniques to follow and actions to be taken to put you on the path to success.

You must take responsibility for your life if you want to make it a better one. While it is not complicated, it takes belief, dedication, and effort. Some setbacks are normal, but how you process and respond to those setbacks is an indicator of your external success. Your positive reaction will be another building block to your eventual success. Some failure is actually a vital component of building towards your success. How you address those setbacks is key to connecting your expectations and performance. You must take personal responsibility for your own actions and persevere by keeping your goals in the forefront. You will learn that *by working the process and following through with effort, anything is achievable.*

The path to personal leadership is neither a quick solution nor a mini-course in self-improvement. It is not sufficient to perform some of the Steps and not others. You must follow this systematic process for the rest of your life. Systematically, it is a new way of life. Through this process, you will examine your life and become cognizant of your current situation. Time will be spent on acquiring a knowledge and understanding of your Guiding Principles, which will help to explain why you do things a certain way. Knowing what it is you want to accomplish and constructing a plan are necessary steps in achieving the desired results. Rounding out the steps are items that reinforce and support what you will need to do including taking time for yourself. The process, when applied daily, is the approach that makes the process work successfully.

> *"If you could get up the courage to begin, you have the courage to succeed."* — **David Viscott**

You need to be ready to learn and make the necessary changes happen.

> *"When the student is ready, the teacher will arrive."*
> — **Anonymous**

ACTION ITEM 1: It will be necessary for you to keep a *NOTEBOOK* or *JOURNAL* in which you will write and compile all the information, thoughts, ideas, and actions you have as you progress down this path. The notebook can be bound, loose-leaf, computer, or PDA whichever may be your preference. Other useful tools can be your computer's PIM (personal information manager), or a planner such as DayRunner™, Franklin Planner™, or one for your PDA. The preference is to strive towards a paperless effort. Another useful tool is to have some type of voice recorder to capture ideas when you are on the move. Whatever approach you choose, be organized and perform the daily activity to document your steps, thoughts, and plans. The act of writing in the book will serve three purposes:

1. it will help you to simplify & clarify your thoughts,
2. it will become a written statement that your subconscious mind will recognize as "truth", and
3. it provides a documented history of the improvements you have made in your life.

Begin your journal work by creating a list of your dreams and desires (next page has a worksheet entitled "Desires" you can use). Try to remember that when you were a child, you allowed your mind to run freely without restrictions or boundaries. Take that approach to create your list of desires. As you go through the steps, you will evaluate your current situation, understand your guiding principles, establish goals, and put those into a prioritized list. Develop and work your plan of action.

DESIRES

List those things you long or hope for to fulfill your dreams. Allow your mind to run free without restrictions or boundaries.   **Date:** __/____

Your notebook will become a record of your personal growth. It will contain everything important to your growth. The information will support your efforts and enable you to become a winner. It is here that you will document and be reminded of your guiding principles, your vision, etc. Eventually it will contain pages that record the following information: your Desires, Guiding Principles, Vision, Mission, Goals (5 year, 3 year, & 1 year), To-Dos, Affirmations, Inspirational Quotes, Accomplishments, Winning Ways steps, and Self-Evaluations. Also, there is a Workbook available to provide notebook size worksheets for your use.

Your positive attitude towards your ability to achieve your potential is a key point. If you are willing to spend the time to create a plan and exert the necessary effort to make it happen, I can teach you the techniques so

YOU CAN LIVE LIFE YOUR WAY!

You are on your way. You have begun the program, which will put you on the path to being able to live your life your way. An old Chinese proverb states:

> *"A journey of a thousand miles begins with a single step."* - **Lao-Tzu** (604BC-531BC)

"He who looks outside dreams, he who looks inside awakens." - Carl Jung

Step 1

SELF-AWARENESS (WHO AM I?)

> *"An unexamined life is not worth living."* — Plato, Apology
> and
> *"Who in the world am I? Ah, that's the great puzzle."* — Lewis Carroll

As you begin your journey, you must first know and understand your starting point and what resources are available. In this step, you will:

- learn more about your current status and who you are;
- analyze your career from both where you are and what your aspirations are;

- examine your relationships with family, friends, and other community relationships;
- understand how you fit into this world;
- know what resources you have available to assist you in achieving your aspirations.

There are questions that you are about to answer that will help you to take stock of yourself. The answers may or may not surprise you; however, it will provide you with a baseline understanding of who you are. You will know:

- What are your skills?
- What are your accomplishments?
- What is most important to you?
- What gives your life meaning?
- What do you want to be? And
- What do you want to do with your life?

GETTING TO KNOW YOURSELF

Whole Brain Thinking

The human brain is comprised of two connected hemispheres, commonly referred to as the left-brain and the right brain. Each hemisphere is specialized for certain behaviors and they operate in different contexts. The majority of people are right handed and the left-brain is primarily detail oriented, while the right is visually oriented and recognizes patterns. The right hemisphere recognizes the picture, the overview or the context, while the left-brain translates that image into words. When you look at a person who seems to be someone you knew a long time ago, you recognize the pattern of that person's face long before his or her name catches up. You move in for a closer look, while trying not to stare, and your left-brain is thinking, "Oh, that's um, oh...I'll never forget, um, what's his name."

The detail-oriented, left-brain hemisphere provides these functions:

- Mathematics
- Logic
- Sequential perception
- Rational analysis
- Precision
- Translation of visual images from the right side of the brain into words.

The pattern-recognizing, right-brain hemisphere provides these functions:
- Spatial awareness
- Holistic or Whole picture
- an "Artistic" ability utilizing visual imagery
- Musical ability
- Memory
- Emotions
- Intuitive impressions.

Everyone uses both sides of the brain, but most people usually have a dominant side. The testing and approaches used will utilize one side of the brain or the other. You will learn which side of your brain is dominant or utilized more often. This insight will help you to better understand yourself and the exercises you will do will work both sides, thus helping you to become more able to jump from one type of skill set to another.

The Approach

The first step in the process of developing your goals and plans is to become totally self-aware of who, what, and where you are. If you were trying to visit me but had never been to my house, you might contact me to ask directions. Before I could provide you with those directions, I would ask you where you would be coming from or where are you now. I could not begin to provide directions unless I first knew your starting point. In order to get anywhere, we must know where we are so that we could chart a course for this journey.

Many people looking to become winners miss this very important first step. They might know where they want to go but, they aren't willing to take the time or put in the effort to find out where they are now. Something so basic is often ignored. These people do not or will not ask themselves the really hard questions nor do they face their true personality and behavior characteristics. They do not address the real issues that undermine their activities and efforts to succeed. You must acknowledge these facets of yourself that are affecting your life and learn how to deal with them.

Why go through all this work? How will you accomplish it? To help put this step into perspective, think about the meaning of the following quote:

> *"Only barbarians are not curious about where they come from, how they came to be where they are, where they appear to be going, whether they wish to go there, and if so, why, and if not, why not."* — **Isaiah Berlin,** English Philosopher 1909-1997

There are different approaches that you can take to begin your personal self-awareness journey. This book will enable you to put into motion your efforts and provide some of the tools to perform the analysis. We will look at a few different techniques that each will provide different insights necessary to help you determine your current reality. This first step is tremendously important in that it provides the foundation upon which to build the following steps to become a winner.

As you utilize the following techniques, you will examine your life and develop a better understanding of where you are, why you are there, and how your personal characteristics mold the results. The attention to this detail will remove any "blind-spots", enable you to understand your actions, and attend to correcting or modifying unwanted behaviors. This effort sets up your self-awareness and is the foundation of your new future.

Remember, a good and stable foundation provides the base upon which you will build your future.

Devote the time necessary to understand and apply the techniques presented. Later in this chapter you will find the questionnaire to conduct your own personal inventory of your skills and abilities.

MASLOW'S NEEDS HIERARCHY

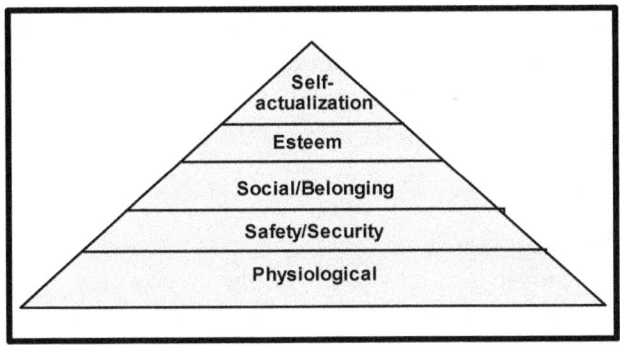

Abraham Maslow is known for his theory of a hierarchy of needs. He writes that human beings are motivated by unsatisfied needs, and that certain lower needs must be satisfied before higher needs can be satisfied. According to Maslow, there are general types of needs (physiological, safety, social, and esteem) that must be satisfied before a person can act selflessly. He called these needs "deficiency needs or D-needs." As long as we are motivated to satisfy these cravings, we are growing and moving towards self-actualization, which is the highest motivating force to reach the ultimate human potential.

Once a need level is being satisfied, other higher needs emerge i.e. safety rather than physiological needs dominate. When these are satisfied, new and still higher needs emerge. As one type of need is satisfied, another pops up to take its place. We can describe this hierarchy of needs depicted in the pyramid above as follows:

Physiological Needs
Physiological needs are the very basic needs such as air, water, food, sleep, sex, etc. When these are not satisfied we may feel sickness, irritation, pain, discomfort, etc. These feelings motivate us to alleviate them as soon as possible to establish a state of relative equilibrium. Once the need is satisfied, we are able to think about other things.

Safety/Security Needs
When we have taken care of the physiological needs, this second layer of needs comes into play. Safety needs have to do with establishing stability and consistency in a chaotic world. These needs are mostly psychological in nature. You will become increasingly interested in finding safe circumstances, stability, and protection.

Social/Belonging Needs
When physiological needs and safety needs are by-and-large taken care of, a third layer starts to emerge. Love and belongingness are the next level of needs. Humans have a desire to belong to groups: family, religious groups, gangs, clubs, work groups, etc. We need to feel loved by others and/or accepted by others. We begin to feel the need for friends, a sweetheart, a desire to marry, have a family, be a part of a community, a member of a church, a brother in the fraternity, a part of a gang or a bowling club. It is also a factor in what we look for in a career.

Esteem Needs
At the next level, we begin to look for esteem. Maslow noted two versions of esteem needs, a lower one and a higher one. The lower one is the need for the attention and recognition that comes from others, the need for status, fame, glory, reputation, appreciation, dignity, even dominance. The higher form involves the need for respect, including such feelings as confidence, competence, achievement, mastery, independence, freedom, and self-respect. Note that this is the "higher" form because, unlike the respect of others, once you have self-respect, it is a lot harder to lose.

Self-Actualization
The last level is a bit different. Maslow called it "being needs or B-needs" (in contrast to D-needs), or self-actualization, which is the term most popularly used. Once the other lower level needs are satisfied, you can begin to maximize your potential. The need for self-actualization is to become everything that you are capable of becoming. It is the need to maximize your potential. You can seek knowledge, peace, esthetic experiences, self-fulfillment, and oneness with God. Once these self-actualization needs are engaged, they continue to be felt. In fact, they are likely to become stronger as we feed them. They involve the continuous desire to *"be all that you can be"* hence the term, self-actualization.

Dr. C. George Boeree, a retired professor of psychology, at his web-site discussing Abraham Maslow, "http://www.ship.edu/~cgboeree/maslow.html, Copyright 1998. 2006 by C. George Boeree" discusses Maslow and specifically self-actualization in more detail and gets into the characteristics of self-actualizing people. If you would like a more in-depth elaboration on Self-Actualization, I would recommend going to his site and reading it.

Other Needs Approaches
Dr. Murray Banks, a 1930's psychologist, explored another theory examining human needs and stated that humans have four basic needs, health, love, variety, and respect. Rather than discuss the needs as levels to be achieved, he looked at them as fitting into four simple classifications. Franklin Covey in its "Reality Model" further defined this approach. The needs are describe as:

- The need to *live* – which is basic, physical survival and the ability to live.
- The need to *love* – which is the desire for intimate relationships.
- The need for *variety* – which is the way we make our lives interesting and fun.

- The need for *self-worth* – which gives meaning to our lives by defining who we are and how we are perceived.

Dr. Gerald Bell, a noted professor at University of North Carolina at Chapel Hill and motivational speaker, discovered the same type of concerns. He conducted a survey, of 4,000 retired executives with an average age of 70, asking them "If you could live your life over, what would you do differently?" These executives who are all very successful by most standards responded about:

- Taking better care of their health
- Working on family goals a lot more
- Spending more time on personal development and career planning
- Giving more time to the community and spiritual matters.

Each of these approaches describes the human needs that must be understood, articulated, and fulfilled in order to complete our lives.

PERSONAL INVENTORY

A personal inventory needs to be conducted, that is, an analysis of where you are now. One of the reasons this is not done by most people is that they do not want to face the reality of their circumstances. They think it is worse than it is; however, it's always better to face reality. It takes courage, but the reward is well worth facing your fears.

Another reason that it is not done is that people do not understand the importance of conducting the personal inventory to establish a good foundation upon which to build. Instead, they flit from item to item that they believe is important, without a plan or ever completing a project to achieve the desired outcome. This approach does not specifically allow them to understand their strengths and build from a solid basis. Most of the time they move from one objective to the next too soon, that is, before the new habit is firmly established they have moved on and frequently slip back on the gains that were accomplished. These people are not able to manage their personal growth.

There is a saying "What gets measured gets done." You cannot manage what you do not measure. Conversely, what isn't measured does not get attention. Out of sight is out of mind, but the emotions attached to the condition are always there.

> *"...habit took the advantage of inattention; inclination was sometimes too strong for reason."* —
> **Ben Franklin**, Autobiography

This is not the be-all and end-all for getting a fix on your present position, but it will get you started and help you to set goals and determine priorities for projects. There is no right or wrong answer. Take your inventory and remember, *"What gets measured gets done."*

The major concerns of your life can be grouped into three categories:

1. Personal
    a. Family
    b. Spiritual
    c. Education/Learning
    d. Financial
    e. Health & Well Being
    f. Home & Shelter
2. Career
3. Psychological
    a. Social/Leisure
    b. Community Service
    c. Behavior

PERSONALITY TYPES

Understanding your personality type and style is another aspect of self-discovery. Knowing this information will help you to understand yourself better, your approach to situations, and most importantly your inherent strengths. There is no "best" type, however knowing your personality type will help you to discover what motivates and energizes you and how you tend to interact with others, which provides an understanding of yourself and how to best relate to others.

In addition, your personality reflects the way others perceive and respond to you. Knowing how others perceive you can enable you to interact with them more effectively and allow you to correct any mistaken impressions they may have of you.

There are various ways that you can determine your personality type. You could utilize a self-administered informal assessment or you could have a professional administer the instrument. Another approach is to utilize the internet to find a test vehicle. The more formal testing administered by a trained professional can produce results that are more accurate and additional insights about your personality type.

Once a personality type is formed, it tends to remain consistent. A person's personality traits shape the ease or difficulty one has with tasks presented to them. Mismatch of personality type to the environment can lead to difficult situations. Once you have identified your personality type, you can read the description of the personality profile. Many people will recognize their behaviors and most people will also learn some additional insights. Knowing your personality type will help you to identify your innate strengths, enable you to gain insights, and suggest the environments that are best for you. With this information, you can seek situations that work with your strengths rather than trying to remove your "weaknesses."

ASSESSMENT TESTS

There are a number of resources for the various types of exams or "test instruments." Still recognized are: Myers-Briggs, Strong Interest Inventory, Self-Directed Search, Berkeley Personality Profile or Big Five Personality Test, and some type of 360-degree. A few of the books listed in the bibliography have modified or limited versions of the test instrument. These tests also may be available at some schools, online, or with psychologists who specialize in administering and interpreting the results. You can choose to conduct a limited self-administered review or a full out professionally administered review. Whichever approach you choose, be sure it provides the information you will need to better understand yourself.

Myers-Briggs

The Myers-Briggs Type Indicator (MBTI) is a personality inventory assessment test, that was developed by Katherine Briggs and her daughter Isabel Briggs Myers, based on the work of Carl Jung. The test can be self-administered from a question and answer booklet. The more formal approach is to have it administered and interpreted by a trained and qualified person; however, you can perform informal exercises that will yield reasonable results.

An informal approach is contained in books referenced in the bibliography called "Please Understand Me II," "Do What You Are" and another book is "Type Talk." The first book contains a self-administered test developed by the author, David Keirsey, which helps you to determine your personality type. The assumption made in these books is that you can honestly evaluate your preferences on how you approach aspects of behavior and decision making and that will provide insights in how you can be most effective in your relationships with other people.

One of sixteen four letter codes which are derived from the following four pairs of styles: E/I, S/N, T/F, and J/P defines your personal style, or how you behave most of the time. Distinguishing between each pair can sometimes be difficult, since we tend to exhibit both characteristics of each pair at some time or other.

Extraversion vs. Introversion – This considers where you primarily get and direct your energy. Extraversion refers to people who tend to get energy from interacting with the outside world and collecting information, while introversion refers to people who get their energy from being alone and having sufficient time to think about a situation. People who prefer Extraversion typically are in situations where they work with and socialize with people in an active way. Introversion people typically are in situations where they work alone or spend recreational time alone and where they can spend time quietly reflecting on what they are doing. Everyone generally has some balance of both extroversion and introversion but one or the other will normally increase your energy level while the other approach will decrease it.

Sensing vs. iNtuition – This refers to how you look at the world around you and how you receive and process information. Sensing refers to being reality focused on tangible things based on using your senses of feel, smell, touch, see, and hear to understand what is happening, i.e. observing each individual tree in a forest. These people tend to prefer situations that are more clear-cut and fact-filled. Intuition refers to having some insight or focus on what might be. Using imagination and creative abilities enables one to get the big picture,, i.e. seeing the whole forest. These people tend to make inferences about other people or situations.

Thinking vs. Feeling – This refers to how you prefer to make decisions. When the information has been gathered, the Thinking type person tends to use logical and impersonal analysis to evaluate the situation where there are consistent principles and objective criteria used to treat people impartially. The Feeling type person tends to think about the people and values in making a decision so that primarily, the welfare of the person is taken into account.

Perceiving vs. Judging – This refers to how you live your life, that is, how you deal with the outside world. Judging types tend to prefer to plan and make decisions, and appear to live structured, organized lives. Perceiving types tend to learn as they go, experience new things, and keep their options open, and appear to be spontaneous and flexible and feel most effective without set plans.

As stated above, everyone uses both types of each pair at least some of the time but one type tends to be more natural and automatic and is the preferred type for that person. Knowing and understanding your preferred personality type provides you with an intimate knowledge of how and why you act a certain way and your approach to events around you. Each of us is unique and additional knowledge about ourselves enables us to explore our identity and orient ourselves in this complex world.

Strong Interest Inventory/Self-Directed Search

The Strong Interest Inventory is another assessment instrument. It is a widely used interest inventory instrument and you are defined by a three-letter code. A variation of this assessment tool is called the "Self-Directed Search" developed by Dr. John Holland in 1971. These instruments measure an individual's work and personal interests. The SDS is a self-administered, self-scored, and self-interpreted interest inventory.

You can utilize either of these assessment tests to provide an inventory of vocational interests. They determine your general career interests by comparing your answers to those of a large population of both men and women. These instruments do not measure your ability or aptitude for a particular occupation but rather your interests. Six different types can loosely classify you as follows:

Realistic – types are people who enjoy being outdoors and working with machines, tools, and or animals. They generally possess athletic, mechanical, or manual skills.

Investigative – types are people who like to work independently and think about problems and issues. They generally have strong math, science, and analytical abilities.

Artistic – types are people who avoid regimented and routine activities and prefer settings where they can be creative and imaginative. They generally possess literary, artistic, and or musical skills.

Social – types are people who enjoy helping others and contributing to society. They generally have good interpersonal and communication skills.

Enterprising – types are often people who enjoy interacting with people in a way that involves persuasion, management, and leadership. They generally are competitive, self-confident, and have good decision-making skills.

Conventional – types are people who follow established procedures, understand expectations and prefer structured and organized situations. They generally possess strong verbal and or numerical abilities and make good team members in a routine environment.

Your three-letter code helps to describe your favorite combination of activities and interests. The hexagon depicts the relationship of the six types, with the location of your types providing insights to similar or dissimilar interests. The interest types most similar to each other are arranged next to each other, and those most dissimilar are arranged directly across the hexagon from each other. Therefore, types adjacent such as Investigative and Artistic have much in common. These characteristics can be helpful to identify environments that are more comfortable and beneficial for you.

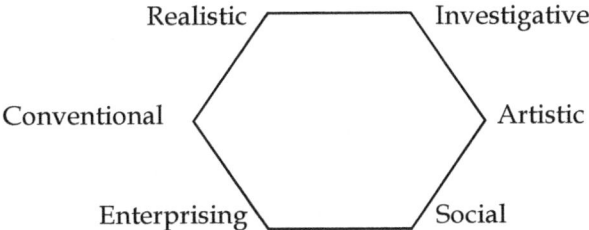

Berkeley Personality Profile

Another instrument is a self-administered, self-interpreted personality assessment called the Berkeley Personality Profile. This approach is considered reflective because it relies on your own insights and those around you rather than an interpretation by a professional test analyzer. Refer to the book entitled "Who Do You Think You Are?" by Harary in the bibliography for more information. It deals with the five basic dimensions of personality, nicknamed the Big Five. The deal with the entire spectrum of each characteristic style following:

- Expressive – covers expressiveness and extraversion through the range to introversion,
- Interpersonal - interpersonal warmth through the total opposite including being cruel,
- Work - approach toward work and other responsibilities covering the range from meeting responsibilities to complete procrastination,
- Emotional - degree of emotional intensity and typical way of dealing with stress,
- Intellectual - engagement in creative and intellectual pursuits from favoring familiar ways to the opposite of preferring original or creative approaches.

In the book "Who Do You Think You Are?"(pg. 16-17), the authors make the point "Research shows that people's personality characteristics with respect to the Big Five dimensions powerfully influence the way they behave and the choices they make. In this way, personality has wide-ranging effects on health and exercise habits, relationships, and career paths."

Johari Window and 360-Degree Feedback

Another type of instrument that can be very useful is one that uses feedback from people around you. Two well-known tests are referred to as the Johari Window" and the "360-degree Feedback." Both use input from people around you to provide an external view, which may be very different from your own view. It removes the "blind-sided" approach that you may have to understanding yourself.

Wikipedia provides the following information "A Johari window is a cognitive psychological tool created by Joseph Luft and Harry Ingham in 1955 in the United States, used to help people better understand their interpersonal communication and relationships." By describing yourself from a fixed list of adjectives, then asking your friends and colleagues to describe you from the same list enables the creation of a grid of overlap and difference. The information about you relates to behaviors, attitudes, emotions, feelings, knowledge, skills, experience, etc. The Johari Window presents the results in one of four windows as follows:

Johari Window

	Known to Self	Unknown to Self
Known To Others	**1** Open Arena	**2** Blind Spot
Unknown To Others	**3** Facade	**4** Unknown

The standard way to depict the information is to show the four windows as equal in size. Window 1 represents the "open area" that is known by all and is the basis of our dealings with others. The larger this window is the more effective and productive we are in our dealings with others. These make our communication with others free and open as well as free from confusion and mistrust.

Window 2 is our "blind spot." It is that area we do not recognize yet others know. Window 3 is the area of our life that we do not want to expose to others. For some people, it enables them to be devious in their dealings with others. Window 4 is a hidden area from everyone, including ourselves. The smaller this area is the better off we are.

Wikipedia describes the "360-degree feedback, also known as multi-rater feedback, multisource feedback, or multisource assessment, is feedback that comes from all around an employee...Feedback is provided by subordinates, peers, and supervisors. It also includes a self-assessment and, in some cases, feedback from external sources such as customers and suppliers or other interested stakeholders."

When you go to the internet (it is assumed that everyone has access either at home or through their local public library), you need to be careful as to what you are getting. There is a lot of free information and tests as well as some sites that may well be less helpful. You can search and find many sites that have good, useful information and tests, such as:

Career and Personality Tests Online for a fee
http://www.discoveryourpersonality.com/index.html
http://www.discoveryourpersonality.com/testlist.html

http://www.cpp.com/company/index.asp

Myers-Briggs free personality test and info
http://sminds.com/mbti/
http://www.teamtechnology.co.uk/mb-intro/mb-intro.htm

Keirsey Temperament (free testing and similar to MBTI
http://www.keirsey.com/
http://www.keirsey.com/sorter/register.aspx

http://www.myersbriggs.org/

Psychology Today Magazine covers Berkeley Personality Profile http://www.psychologytoday.com/articles/200910/the-ptberkeley-personality-test

One web site to obtain information about the Johari Window is: http://kevan.org/johari

YOUR CURRENT REALITY

After reading and working through each of the previous self-awareness sections, you have input as to where you are in a personal sense and how you may have arrived. There is no right or wrong answer, only answers to the questions. Using the Myers-Briggs indicator, you will have one of 16 fundamental personality type profiles. These are indicators of how you approach, look at, evaluate, and react to issues. For example, a result of Extraverted, iNtuitive, Thinking, and Perceiving (ENTP) provides an understanding into a personality that is enthusiastic, ingenious, resourceful, and energetic.

The Self Directed Search provides you with indications of your three highly used interest areas. These can provide additional insights to occupations and activities that are compatible to your personality type. For example, a result of INVESTIGATIVE, ARTISTIC, and REALISTIC provides some guidance as to the general types of occupations that interest you. Your response to the Needs Assessment coupled with the Personal Inventory provides additional information.

When you have completed your self-analysis, you should have seen a pattern and recognized your dominant tendencies. Are you a thinker who analyzes everything or a feeler who relies on gut-instinct? These tendencies provide the same way of responding to a situation repeatedly. As each situation arises, your personality type, experience, knowledge, and environment will all come into play and influence the outcome. It becomes a habit. We must continue or change so that the path leads us to real growth and not self-destruction.

WOTS UP ANALYSIS

Modern business analysis calls for a type of analysis commonly referred to as a SWOT analysis. It requires that the business review its Strengths and Weaknesses and then its Opportunities and Threats. If we change the order of the letters to WOTS and add the word "Up", we have a phrase and acronym that is easy to remember and more importantly, reminds us of what it is we are trying to accomplish at this point in time.

We can take this important and useful concept and apply it to our personal lives. By understanding your weaknesses, you can manage and/or eliminate threats that might otherwise stifle you. With some introspective time, we can begin to understand "WOTS Up" in our lives and capitalize on our talents and abilities. Think about each category (it really doesn't matter in what order) and answer the questions:

Weaknesses – limitations or negative attributes:
- What criticisms have you received?
- What are your main limitations?
- What are your negative work habits (for example, are you often late, are you disorganized, do you have a short temper, or are you poor at handling stress)?
- What tasks do you usually avoid because you don't feel confident doing them?
- What education / skills / abilities do you believe are needed that you do not have?
- Do you have personality traits that hold you back? For instance, if you have a position that requires customer interface, a dislike of public interaction would be a major weakness.
- What were your failures when you tried but did not achieve your goals?
- What caused them to be failures?

Opportunities – positive external events you can potentially leverage:

- What dreams, wishes or goals have you been considering?
- What new technology can help you? Can you get help from others or from people via the Internet?
- How can you utilize your strengths to take advantage of the current market?
- Do you have a strong network of strategic contacts that may help you, or offer good advice?
- What trends do you see, and how can you take advantage of them?
- Were there opportunities that you missed?
- What chances should you have taken
- List a few people you admire most and indicate what you consider the key factor to their success.

Threats/Constraints – uncontrollable external factors that you may be able to overcome or avoid:

- What obstacles do you currently face in your everyday life or at work?
- Does changing technology threaten your position?
- Are any of your colleagues competing with you for projects or roles?
- Is your job or the demand for the things you do, changing?
- Could any of your weaknesses lead to or increase the level of these threats or the impact they can have on you?

Strengths – positive attributes and talents

- Which of your achievements are you most proud of?
- What made them successes?
- What skills / abilities / special talents that contributed to or caused the success?
- What motivated you to succeed?

Step 1 - Self-Awareness

- What advantages do you have that others don't have (for example, skills, certifications, education, or connections)?
- What values do you believe in that others fail to exhibit?
- Are you part of a network that no one else is involved in? What connections do you have with influential people?
- What do you do better than anyone else?
- What personal resources can you access?
- What do other people see as your strengths?

Take sufficient time to complete the analysis of your strengths and weaknesses as well as the opportunities and threats that you face. Add other pertinent questions and answers for each of the four areas that you deem useful. Reflect upon what the answers are telling you about yourself. What do you see? Is there a pattern or an issue that stands out for you to address? This effort helps you focus on your strengths, minimize your weaknesses, and take the greatest possible advantage of opportunities available to you. You should now have a better understanding as to WOTS Up.

ACTION ITEM 2: Find a quiet place where you are free from interruptions. Schedule the time necessary to answer the questions in the following Personal Inventory; then review and examine your answers. This effort will take some time to accomplish. Be prepared and do not rush through the effort. The examination of the data, mulling over the whys and wherefores, will provide you with an understanding of your baseline or starting point for the rest of your life.

Upon completing these analyses, you should spend time examining the results and exert the effort to understand them. You should be thinking about the answers to questions such as:

- What weaknesses do you need to improve upon?

- What weaknesses do you need to manage so they do not become impediments?
- What opportunities should you pursue?
- What threats do you need to work on to eliminate or at least minimize?
- What strengths can you make stronger?
- What strengths you can use to enhance your pursuit of your goals?

Be aware that the human psyche is very complex and each person is unique. We may have dominant traits but we also consist of characteristics of other traits. The results are not black and white but contain many shades of gray. Use these guidelines to develop an in-depth understanding of who you are. When you have developed an understanding, write a paragraph or two describing who you are. For example:

> *"I am a person who enjoys people. I have many roles from spouse to friend and neighbor, to associate. I have two young children and I enjoy spending time with my spouse and the children. I enjoy being around people and having interesting and lively discussions on various topics.*
>
> *I can summarize my working career as being a manager with abilities managing and motivating teams, and in building partnerships. I possess the ability to chose, lead, hire, fire, motivate, and mentor groups of individuals. I've achieved significant cost savings, exceeded performance objectives, created and improved processes, and motivated staff to maximize productivity and bottom line results. I have international experience, building start-ups, managing through bankruptcy, and managing in Fortune 100 companies. My strengths include being a skilled problem solver capable of managing the "big picture" across multiple disciplines. "*

YOUR PERSONAL INVENTORY

Date: __/__

(Your Personal Inventory questionnaire, originally developed by Michael E. Angier [Copyright 2000, Success Networks International Inc.], used with permission and has been modified for our use.)

General

What accomplishments do I feel especially good about having completed?

_____
_____
_____

What are my 3 most significant accomplishments?

_____
_____
_____

If I could, what life situations would I want to repeat?

_____
_____
_____

What is going very well for me right now?

_____
_____
_____

What are the three biggest challenges I am now facing and struggling with to achieve?

_____
_____

When I am working on a project or a problem, am I open to new ideas or approaches to find a solution?

YES	NO

My three most important current projects are:
_____
_____
_____

My three most important goals for the next year are:
_____
_____
_____

My three most important goals for the next five years are:
_____
_____
_____

My three most important goals for the next ten years are:
_____
_____
_____

I want to develop the following habits:
_____
_____
_____

What am I tolerating in my life that I no longer wish to tolerate?
_____
_____
_____

YOUR NEEDS HIERARACHY LEVEL

Maslow's Needs Hierarchy

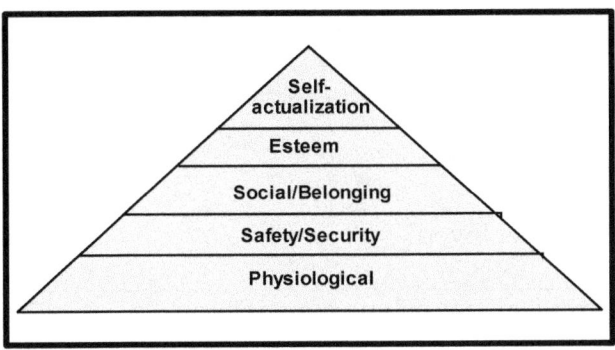

Physiological Needs:

Do you have enough food and water to survive?	Yes	No
Do you have a place to live?	Yes	No
Do you have clothing to keep you warm?	Yes	No

Safety/Security Needs:

Do you feel safe?	Yes	No
Do you feel emotionally secure?	Yes	No
Do you have stability in your life?	Yes	No

Social/Belonging Needs:

Do you feel loved?	Yes	No
Do you feel you belong somewhere?	Yes	No
Do you belong to an organization or group?	Yes	No

Esteem Needs:

Do you receive the attention you deserve?	Yes	No
Do you feel good about yourself?	Yes	No
Do you feel worthwhile as a human being?	Yes	No

Self-Actualization:

Do you feel accomplished?	Yes	No
Do you feel fulfilled?	Yes	No
Do you feel at peace with yourself and the world?	Yes	No

Now that you understand each level, place yourself on the triangle at the level that you believe you need to address. Recognize that it is very common to be working issues at more than one level at a time. However, once a level is totally completed then you can step out of it onto the next level up the pyramid. Are you still attending to your physiological needs? Do you have enough of your basic needs to survive? If your answer is NO, you must continue to work to take care of your basic physiological needs to survive. If your answer is YES, continue to look up the triangle, assessing your status at each level until you reach the level that you must continue to work at to satisfy your needs. This assessment will provide you with a baseline in your self-awareness analysis.

Write a paragraph to describe your status. For Example:

"My physiological needs are taken care of. Both my education and my experience provide me with the tools necessary to work and earn a wage that is sufficient to take care of those needs. I have been with the same person for X years and we have a great relationship supporting each other in our personal endeavors. While I feel good about our relationship, I feel there is more I can do to belong to my community. There is some type of void that must be filled in order for me to feel comfortable within the social/belonging arena."

Now it is your turn.

_____
_____
_____
_____
_____
_____
_____
_____
_____

Personal

Family

What do I need from my family?
_____
_____

My relationship with my spouse is:
- ❏ Blissful
- ❏ Very happy
- ❏ Happy
- ❏ Unhappy

My relationship with my children is:
- ❏ Extremely close
- ❏ Warm
- ❏ Strained
- ❏ Non-existent

My relationship with my siblings is:
- ❏ Extremely close
- ❏ Warm
- ❏ Strained
- ❏ Non-existent

My relationship with my parents is:
- ❏ Extremely close
- ❏ Warm
- ❏ Strained
- ❏ Non-existent

What do I want to do with or for my family?
_____
_____

What am I tolerating in family life that I no longer wish to tolerate?
_____
_____

Spiritual

My level of satisfaction with my spiritual life is:
- ❏ Very pleased
- ❏ Satisfied
- ❏ So-so
- ❏ Very dissatisfied

My relationship with my Higher Power is:
- ❏ Very close
- ❏ Satisfying
- ❏ So-so
- ❏ Non-existent

I pray or meditate:
- ❏ Regularly
- ❏ Less than I should
- ❏ Rarely
- ❏ Never

I have a current mission statement that reflects my highest values.

YES	NO

My spiritual needs are:
_____
_____
_____

I feel I am out of integrity in the following places:
_____
_____
_____

What am I tolerating that I no longer wish to tolerate?
_____
_____
_____

Educational/Learning

I have the following educational credentials / certifications / degrees:
_____
_____

I want to earn the following
degrees/certifications/credentials:
_____
_____

I'm currently studying the following:
_____
_____

I rate my technological knowledge as:

❑ techno geek ❑ savvy
❑ average user ❑ clueless

I want to learn more (skills, knowledge, etc.) about:
_____
_____

I daydream seeing myself doing:
_____
_____

What am I tolerating in the area that I no longer wish to tolerate?
_____
_____

Financial

My current monthly income is $_____.

My present net worth (assets minus liabilities) is $_____.

My happiness with my financial status is:
  ❑ very pleased   ❑ satisfied
  ❑ so-so   ❑ unhappy

I have $_____.in my retirement portfolio.

I currently save/invest $_____ per month.

What are my different streams of income?
_____
_____
_____

Status of bills/taxes etc.:
  ❑ All current   ❑ Usually behind
  ❑ Occasionally behind ❑ Almost always late

I have an up-to-date will/trust. | YES | NO |

My financial records are orderly and up-to-date. | YES | NO |

What is my dream of my financial position?
_____
_____
_____

What am I tolerating in the area that I no longer wish to tolerate?
_____
_____
_____

Health & Well Being

My current weight is _____.

My ideal weight is _____

My cholesterol is _____.

My body fat percentage is _____.

My blood pressure is _____.

My last complete physical was _____.

I have the following ailments:

_____   _____

_____   _____

Overall rating for my current health status:
- ❏ excellent
- ❏ good
- ❏ fair
- ❏ poor

I wear my seat belt:
- ❏ 100% of the time
- ❏ 75% of the time
- ❏ 50% of the time
- ❏ 0% of the time

I drink alcohol:
- ❏ Much to excess
- ❏ Occasionally
- ❏ Seldom
- ❏ Never

I sleep:
- ❏ Very well
- ❏ Well most nights
- ❏ OK most nights
- ❏ I have trouble sleeping

I would rate my diet as:
- ❏ Healthy food in appropriate quantities
- ❏ Good
- ❏ Fair
- ❏ Mainly Junk Food

I exercise:
- ❏ Adequately & consistently
- ❏ Inconsistently
- ❏ Rarely
- ❏ I am a couch potato

What am I tolerating in the area that I no longer wish to tolerate?

_____
_____
_____

Home & Shelter

How I feel about my home:
- ❏ love it
- ❏ happy
- ❏ satisfied
- ❏ very dissatisfied

My home is:
- ❏ Well-organized
- ❏ Fairly well-organized
- ❏ Needs real attention
- ❏ It's a disaster

My dream home is (describe in detail):

_____
_____
_____

What am I tolerating in the area that I no longer wish to tolerate?

_____
_____

Career

My current position is
_____

My happiness and fulfillment with my job or business is:
- ❑ extremely fulfilling   ❑ very happy
- ❑ satisfied   ❑ unhappy
- ❑ terribly unhappy

My next position is
_____

The best job I ever had is/was:
_____
_____
_____

The reason(s) it was the best job is:
_____
_____
_____

What is my dream position? Describe in detail.
_____
_____
_____

My mentor is
_____

What am I tolerating at work that I no longer wish to tolerate?
_____
_____
_____

Psychological

Social

I am happier being:

☐ alone   ☐ with others

My social needs are:
_____
_____
_____

I belong to the following social group(s):
Church_____
Club_____
Organization_____
Other_____

I would describe my circle of friends as (check all that apply):
☐ Extensive
☐ Stimulating
☐ Satisfactory
☐ Supportive
☐ Limited
☐ I'm really unhappy with the number of friends I have

I consider my wardrobe to be:

☐ Excellent   ☐ Good
☐ Fair   ☐ Shabby

What quality of life results do I desire that are different from what I have in this area?
_____
_____
_____

What am I tolerating that I no longer wish to tolerate?
_____
_____
_____

Leisure

What are the sports that I enjoy playing?
_____
_____
_____

I play my sport(s):
    ❑ Often   ❑ Occasionally   ❑ Never

I currently vacation _____ weeks/year.

My automobile is a _____
                    (year & model)

❑ I love my car   ❑ I'm happy with it
❑ I'm ok with it   ❑ Very dissatisfied

What am I tolerating in the area that I no longer wish to tolerate?
_____
_____
_____

Community Service

I volunteer approximately _____ hours a year.

I'm active in my community:
    ❑ Very active   ❑ Moderately active
    ❑ Less than I'd like   ❑ Not at all

What would I like to do differently in this area?

_____
_____
_____

Behavior

	YES	NO
I see humor in everyday life.		
I am able to delegate authority.		
I trust my gut reactions.		
I am comfortable with ambiguity.		
I make decisions based on analysis and not risk of failure.		
I thrive on change.		
I enjoy a challenge.		
When under stress, I focus on solving rather than blaming.		
I usually feel even tempered in stressful circumstances.		
There is more to life than I'm currently experiencing.		
I wonder about my purpose in life.		
I spend time in solitude.		
I reflect on things that provide meaning to my life.		

YOUR PERSONALITY TYPE

Your Myers-Briggs four letter code is: __ __ __ __.

Using the Self-Directed Search, you can be defined as: __ __ __.

Step 1 - Self-Awareness

Using the Berkeley Personality Profile, you can define your profile styles as:

Expressive: _____

_____
_____
_____
_____

Interpersonal: _____

_____
_____
_____
___
_____

Work: _____

_____
_____
_____
_____

Emotional: _____

_____
_____

_____

_____

_____

Intellectual:_____

_____

_____

_____

_____

By answering the self-awareness questions honestly, you have documented your status. Find a quiet area and do not rush the review and analysis of your answers as this will be the foundation that you will build upon.

Group the information into the Strengths, Weaknesses, Opportunities, and Threats/Constraints categories (see WOTS Up table on next page). Is this what you expected? Are you satisfied with your result thus far?

Take time to answer the question "Where do you want to go from here?" More detail about this topic will be addressed when we discuss Vision and Mission in Step 4 and then Goal Setting in Step 5.

WOTS UP

Using the questions on pages 67-69, develop your list of items that belong in each category and record them. Once the exercise is completed, use the information to gain additional insights about your status and what activities you can do to move toward your destination.   **Date:** ___/_____

WEAKNESSES (List your limitations in you or in your resources.)	OPPORTUNITIES (How can you take advantage of your strengths? What are areas for improvement for you?)	THREATS/ CONSTRAINTS (What could affect you negatively? What obstacles are in your way?)	STRENGTHS (List your skills, abilities, and special talents. Indicate any resources you may have.)

Now that you have established the fundamentals of your self-awareness assessment, you should have a better understanding of who you are, what skills and abilities you bring to the table, and an indication of where you want to be in the future. Now it is time to take the next step and examine and understand your Guiding Principles.

"Important principles may, and must, be inflexible." - Abraham Lincoln

Step 2

GUIDING PRINCIPLES (MY BELIEFS)

> *"To thine own self be true, and it must follow, as the night the day, thou canst not then be false to any man."* — William Shakespeare, Polonius in Hamlet

As we point ourselves towards a new path, we must know and understand our personal values and principles. If you do not know who you are and what you believe in, your journey through life will be full of distractions which will add stress to your life. Your journey through life will be easier when you have a clear understanding of your values and principles and you live and act in harmony with them.

Having this clarity on what really matters to you and knowing what you believe in will direct you on your journey and enable you to live your life to your fullest potential. Whenever you are faced with a tough decision, you can think of your Guiding Principles and they will provide the answer as to what to do for a given situation. Living a life that is true to your belief system will enable you to make choices that will lead towards real success and you will not regret those choices later in life.

By identifying, clarifying, and focusing on our personal values and guiding principles, we will become more self-aware and consequently have the ability to:

- set up a strong foundation to build upon,
- establish a solid core,
- clarify our boundaries,
- enable rapid decision making,
- assist us in becoming more self-aware,
- facilitate greater integrity,
- permit us to utilize time more effectively,
- make possible a greater capability to achieve our goals, and
- help us to become **winners** in living our lives.

First, we need to come to terms with our belief system.

DEFINITIONS

What is it that we deem as our fundamental guiding principles? Beginning on page 102 is a list of descriptive words (*Qualities, Virtues, Values,* and *Guiding Principles*). Before we begin to clarify our guiding principles, let us first define some terms that are frequently used. The Glossary at the back of the book provides more detailed definitions. When we understand what these terms mean, we can avoid confusion and focus on the desired outcome.

- ➤ Qualities - character or nature, as belonging to or distinguishing a thing.
- ➤ Virtues - moral excellence; goodness; righteousness.
- ➤ Values - worthwhile standard or quality; an established ideal of life.
- ➤ Ethics - a set of moral principles; a theory or system of moral values.
- ➤ Principles - a rule or code of conduct; a truth that is the foundation for other truths.

GUIDING PRINCIPLES

Even if we are not consciously aware of them, every person has a set of guiding principles. Developing clarity of your deepest held values in the three **key** areas of your life, Personal, Career, and Psychological, is essential to putting your life in order. A value system is an organized set of guiding principles that provides guidance along a continuum of relative importance.

Now let us examine guiding principles. If we think of a guiding principle as a *deeply held driving force, a rule of action or conduct, a foundation for our actions, a core belief, and highest priority*, we will find that they define boundaries and govern our mode of conduct. It is something we consider as high truth, and, that for which we will take a stand. Our Guiding Principles are the basis by which we decide what is right and wrong and work to form our unique character.

Origination

You might ask, "Where do my guiding principles come from?" The answer could be from nowhere or from everywhere. While your guiding principles are developed over your lifetime, most are built on what you learned from your parents, religion, teachers, and other influential people in your life. Others come from reading and contemplation, and your life experiences form the rest of the foundation. All these inputs help you to develop your own guiding principles.

Benefits:

If you do not know your values, you will tend to vacillate and be unable to make proper decisions. You will move along without clear direction. These Guiding Principles are the basis of which we will decide what is right or wrong behavior and will enable us to:

- become more self-aware, understand our values and know what we are striving towards;
- prioritize our tasks so that we can decide what comes first;
- make ethical decisions we can live with; and
- become better people who are true to ourselves.

One should not compromise their guiding principles. Once guiding principles are compromised, your journey will take a different path and a "do over" will not take one back to the original path. Comprising ones' guiding principles will result in be a need to work harder to get oneself close to the original pathway.

People familiar with Scouting should immediately recognize that the Scout Oath and Scout Law are guiding principles to help guide our children. A set of principles teach the scouts guidelines for their every action; however, it goes beyond that. Properly taught and worked on during their time as Scouts, it becomes an ingrained behavior and approach to life.

Although the Boy Scouts of America and Girl Scouts of the United States of America operate separate and independent of one another, both have similar Scout Oath/Promise and Scout Law that teaches behavioral skills that last throughout one's lifetime. Here are the Girl Scout Promise and Law. Used with Permission from the Girl Scouts of the United States of America:

> **Girl Scout Promise**
> *On my honor, I will try:*
> *To serve God and my country,*
> *To help people at all times,*
> *And to live by the Girl Scout Law.*

> **Girl Scout Law**
> *I will do my best to be*
> *honest and fair,*
> *friendly and helpful,*
> *considerate and caring,*
> *courageous and strong, and*
> *responsible for what I say and do,*
> *and to*
> *respect myself and others,*
> *respect authority,*
> *use resources wisely,*
> *make the world a better place, and*
> *be a sister to every Girl Scout.*

The more time we spend in sorting out what is important to us, the better we will be at knowing ourselves and strengthening our self-identity and self-assurance. Clear guiding principles will give us a much stronger set of boundaries, thereby facilitating a consciousness of who we are and what we stand for. As a result, we can choose among conflicting opportunities.

Ben Franklin, in his autobiography, described how he created a prioritized list of values and worked on bringing his behavior in line with them.

> *"The Bold and Arduous Project of Arriving at Moral Perfection..."*

> *"It was about this time I conceived the bold and arduous project of arriving at moral perfection. I wished to live without committing any fault at any time; I would conquer all that*

either natural inclination, custom, or company might lead me into. As I knew, or thought I knew, what was right and wrong, I did not see why I might not always do the one and avoid the other. But I soon found I had undertaken a task of more difficulty than I had imagined. While my care was employed in guarding against one fault, I was often surprised by another; habit took the advantage of inattention; inclination was sometimes too strong for reason. I concluded, at length, that the mere speculative conviction that it was our interest to be completely virtuous was not sufficient to prevent our slipping; and that the contrary habits must be broken, and good ones acquired and established, before we can have any dependence on a steady, uniform rectitude of conduct. For this purpose I therefore contrived the following method.

In the various enumerations of the moral virtues I had met with in my reading I found the catalogue more or less numerous, as different writers included more or fewer ideas under the same name. Temperance, for example, was by some confined to eating and drinking, while by others it was extended to mean the moderating every other pleasure, appetite, inclination or passion, bodily or mental, even to our avarice and ambition. I proposed to myself, for the sake of clearness to use rather more names, with fewer ideas annexed to each than a few names with more ideas; and I concluded under thirteen names of virtues all that at that time occurred to me as necessary or desirable and annexed to each a short precept which fully expressed the extent I gave to its meaning.

These names of virtues with their precepts were:

TEMPERANCE - Eat not to dullness; drink not to elevation.

SILENCE - Speak not but what may benefit others or yourself; avoid trifling conversation.

ORDER - Let all your things have their places; let each part of your business have its time.

RESOLUTION - Resolve to perform what you ought; perform

without fail what you resolve.

FRUGALITY - Make no expense but to do good to others or yourself; i.e., waste nothing.

INDUSTRY - Lose no time; be always employed in something useful; cut off all unnecessary actions.

SINCERITY - Use no hurtful deceit; think innocently and justly, and, if you speak, speak accordingly.

JUSTICE - Wrong none by doing injuries or omitting the benefits that are your duty.

MODERATION - Avoid extremes; forbear resenting injuries so much as you think they deserve.

CLEANLINESS - Tolerate no uncleanliness in body, clothes, or habitation.

TRANQUILLITY - Be not disturbed at trifles, or at accidents common or unavoidable.

CHASTITY - Rarely use venery but for health or offspring, never to dullness, weakness, or the injury of your own or another's peace or reputation.

HUMILITY - Imitate Jesus and Socrates.

My intention being to acquire the habitude of all these virtues, I judged it would be well not to distract my attention by attempting the whole at once, but to fix it on one of them at a time; and, when I should be master of that, then to proceed to another, and so on, till I should have gone through the thirteen; and, as the previous acquisition of some might facilitate the acquisition of certain others, I arranged them with that view as they stand above. Temperance first, as it tends to procure that coolness and clearness of head which is so necessary where constant vigilance was to be kept up and guard maintained against the unremitting attraction of ancient habits and the force of perpetual temptations. This being acquired and established, Silence would be more easy; and my desire being to gain knowledge at the same time that I improved in virtue, and considering that in conversation it was obtained rather by the use of the ears than of the tongue, and therefore wishing to break a habit I was getting into of prattling, punning, and joking which only made me acceptable to trifling company, I gave Silence the second place. This and the next, Order, I expected would allow me more time for attending to my project and my studies. Resolution, once become habitual, would keep me firm in my endeavors to obtain all the subsequent virtues; Frugality and Industry freeing me from my remaining debt, and producing affluence and independence, would make more easy the practice of Sincerity and Justice, etc., etc. Conceiving then that agreeably to the advice of Pythagoras in his Golden Verses daily examination would be necessary, I contrived the following method for conducting that examination.

I made a little book, in which I allotted a page for each of the virtues. I ruled each page with red ink so as to have seven columns, one for each day of the week, marking each column with a letter for the day. I crossed these columns with thirteen red lines, marking the beginning of each line with the first letter of one of the virtues, on which line and in its proper column I might mark by a little black spot, every fault I found upon examination to have been committed respecting that virtue upon that day.

I determined to give a week's strict attention to each of the virtues successively. Thus, in the first week, my great guard was to avoid even the least offence against Temperance, leaving the other virtues to their ordinary chance, only marking every evening the faults of the day. Thus, if in the first week I could keep my first line, marked T, clear of spots, I supposed the habit of that virtue so much strengthened and its opposite weakened that I might venture extending my attention to include the next, and for the following week keep both lines clear of spots. Proceeding thus to the last, I could go through a course complete in thirteen weeks and four courses in a year. And like him who, having a garden to weed, does not attempt to eradicate all the bad herbs at once, which would exceed his reach and his strength, but works on one of the beds at a time, and, having accomplished the first, proceeds to a second, so I should have, I hoped, the encouraging pleasure of seeing on my pages the progress I made in virtue by clearing successively my lines of their spots till in the end by a number of courses I should he happy in viewing a clean book after a thirteen weeks' daily examination.

.
.
.

I entered upon the execution of this plan for self-examination, and continued it with occasional intermissions for some time. I was surprised to find myself so much fuller of faults than I had imagined; but I had the satisfaction of seeing them diminish."

It is essential that after you understand your deeply held guiding principles since you live your life based on them. This understanding will result in obtaining self-respect, self-esteem, and self-confidence.

ACTION ITEM 3: This will take some time. Read the remainder of this section and then come back to the action item with your notebook handy. Be prepared to take the time necessary to think about the items you listed and how they fit together.

Ask yourself the following questions:
1. What do I value more than anything else in life?
2. What does my conscience tell me are the highest priorities or values of life?
3. If I could live only three or four guiding principles well, what would they be?

Prepare a list of those principles that guide your life. If you need some help in thinking about your guiding principles, you can use Ben Franklin's items or chose from the list descriptive words below. Further, there are numerous books on philosophy, religion, etc. that may provide guidance for you. Choose whatever source that works for you but be sure to establish your list of guiding principles.

QUALITIES	VIRTUES	VALUES	GUIDING PRINCIPLES
Accurate	Accountable	Achievement	Accountability
Ambitious	Citizenship	Aesthetics	Choice
Balanced	Cleanliness	Awareness	Commitment
Caring	Consecration	Charity	Decisiveness
Collaborative	Contentment	Cheerful	Discipline
Committed	Courage	Community	Duty
Compassionate	Diligence	Compassion	Empathy
Competent	Duty	Contribution	Empowerment
Courageous	Endurance	Courteous	Encouragement
Creative	Faithful	Creativity	Excellence
Credible	Forgiveness	Decisiveness	Fairness
Dependable	Freedom	Dignity	Family
Educated	Fruitfulness	Discipline	Freedom
Enthusiastic	Godliness	Diversity	Frugality
Extroverted	Happiness	Education	Growth
Fair	Holiness	Effort	Health
Faithful	Honorable	Excellence	Honesty
Flexible	Hopeful	Fame	Human dignity
Forgiving	Humility	Family	Humility
Funny	Joyful	Free Time	Integrity
Giving	Kindness	Freedom	Justice
Goodness	Loving	Friendship	Leadership
Helpful	Obedient	Frugality	Learning
Honesty	Patience	Generosity	Love
Industrious	Peacefulness	Growth	Loyalty
Innovative	Perseverance	Happiness	Order
Inspiring	Purity	Health	Patience
Integrity	Resolution	Helpful	Patriotism
Introverted	Reverence	Honesty	Potential
Knowledgeable	Righteousness	Humility	Proactive
Logical	Sincerity	Imagination	Quality
Loving	Steadfastness	Independence	Respect
Loyal	Temperance	Integrity	Responsibility
Moral	Trusting	Justice	Self-discipline

Step 2 - Guiding Principles

Neat	Truthful	Kindness	Self-esteem
Open-minded	Watchfulness	Knowledge	Service
Organized	Zeal	Leadership	Sincerity
Patient		Learning	Spirituality
Powerful		Life	Trustworthiness
Principle-centered		Love	Truth
Proactive		Loyalty	
Receptive		Mentoring	
Respectful		Moderation	
Responsible		Nature	
Self-disciplined		Obedient	
Selfless		Order	
Self-reliant		Passion	
Sensitive		Patriotism	
Thankful		Productivity	
Tolerant		Purpose	
Trustworthy		Relationships	
Truthful		Respect	
Unity		Responsibility	
Visionary		Security	
Wise		Sensitivity	
Witty		Serenity	
		Sincerity	
		Spirituality	
		Stability	
		Teaching	
		Time	
		Tradition	
		Tranquility	
		Truth	
		Wealth	
		Wisdom	
		Working	

This list, while comprehensive, is not necessarily complete but rather a sampling that you can use to assist in the development of your list of guiding principles and vision/mission statements.

After you have this list, write each valued principle as an action statement. For example, if your valued principle was "Honesty," you would now express it as "Be honest."

Make sure they are mutually compatible.

Write a short paragraph to explain and clarify each valued principle. After you have written what they mean, you should have clarity as to how you would use them. See below for examples.

EXAMPLE OF GUIDING PRINCIPLES

COMMIT TO EXCELLENCE.
Maintain the highest integrity in relationships with self, family, friends, and associates. Prepare with goal-directed intensity, maintain image, and never sacrifice quality.

GROW INTELLECTUALLY.
Expand my mind with a depth and breath of reading and thought. Seek discussions that will expand the mind. Weigh all knowledge within the framework of my principles.

HAVE A HIGH SELF-ESTEEM.
Continually develop and maintain a strong sense of personal worth as I relate to myself and others.

LOVE MY FAMILY.
Build a close interpersonal fusion with my spouse and children, showing care, respect, and kindness. Take sufficient meaningful time with them and help each to realize their maximum potential and self-fulfillment.

MAINTAIN EXCELLENT HEALTH.
Avoid anything that will jeopardize my health. Do everything in moderation and exercise regularly.

BE HONEST.
Free myself from any form of hypocrisy. Be open and fair with my family, friends, and associates. See that my dealings are fair, aboveboard, and impeccable with myself and everyone around me.

BE SINCERE.
Approach every situation and person with an open mind. Give all "facts" full consideration and avoid deceit. Speak only what may benefit others or myself; avoid gossip and all meaningless conversations.

BE JUST.
Wrong no one by willful acts or by omission. See that justice is properly administered.

BE A LEADER.
Show the right way by going first and have a following that is voluntary. Guide myself and others with clearly defined, mutually agreed upon goals, and demonstrate the best method of achieving these goals.

BE ORGANIZED.
Let each part of my life have its place and time.

BE FRUGAL.
Waste nothing, especially my time. Always be employed in doing something useful and cut off all unnecessary actions.

BE HUMBLE.
Free myself from boasting, arrogance, egotism, and self-centeredness. Be teachable. Have a close touch with reality and know myself as I really am. Minimize my personal accomplishments in favor of building other people. Imitate Jesus and Socrates.

BE TRANQUIL.
Be serene and composed and do not get overly upset by small issues or accidents.

BE DECISIVE.
Use time effectively to gather and analyze the facts, then make the decision. It will be the best decision at that time.

BE PATIENT.
Wait for the good things in life. They will come with hard work.

If you have not done this yet, establish your list of guiding principles.

GUIDING PRINCIPLES

List your principles that you have decided guide your life. These are the main beliefs by which you live your life.   Date: ___/___

From your list, choose the ten that are the most important to you. After you have your list of ten, eliminate half. Go on the premise that you can only have five guiding principles to live with. Which five would you give up?

You will now have your five most important guiding principles in life. This list will reveal an enormous amount about you. What would you pay for, sacrifice for, suffer for and even die for? What are the guiding principles that you hold most dear? Think these questions through carefully and, when you get a chance, write down your answers. Now imagine that you are only permitted 4. Which one would you give up? Cross it off your list.

Continue to take this approach so that you reduce your list to three, then two. As you look at your last two, decide which one to cross-off. The last remaining guiding principle is the one that is most fundamental to your belief system.

Once you have determined your guiding principles, you should now organize them in order of importance. What is your first, most important guiding principle? Add your second guiding principle, then your third, and so on. This ranking of your guiding principles is one of the very best and fastest ways to define your character and help you to better understand yourself. The more time you spend thinking and writing, the more correct and energizing your guiding principles will become.

Remember, a higher order guiding principle will always take precedence over a lower order one. Whenever you are forced to choose between acting on one guiding principle or another, you always choose the guiding principle that is the highest on your own personal hierarchy. The order or arrangement of your guiding principles can cause a change in your life. A switch in the order can change the way you feel, think, and behave in virtually every area of your life.

YOUR PERSONAL CODE OF CONDUCT

Remember your guiding principles represent your core beliefs and will govern your behavior. Now decide the order your guiding principles need to be for you to be the best person you could possibly be, in order to have the greatest impact or to achieve your ultimate destiny. Too many guiding principles makes it very difficult to manage; focus on your top 3 - 5 guiding principles. Keep working them until they are clear in your mind and daily actions.

ACTION ITEM 4: Evaluate your recent past performance against your guiding principles. Determine which guiding principles are under your control. Where do you lack control in matching your lifestyle with your guiding principles? Bring your performance in line with them.

You should not do this review too quickly. It will take days to sort through the items and get to your basic, core, guiding principles. The more time you can spend contemplating and meditating, the more energized you will become and the more sound your guiding principles will be. Record your results.

Once you have clarified and consciously understood your actions verses your guiding principles, you will have established your personal code of conduct. It is essential that you take the critical step of living by your guiding principles. When you consistently act without hesitation doing the right thing based on your set of guiding principles rather than based on emotion, pressure, instinct, etc., you will have consistency on how you conduct your life.

Most of us will have more demands on us than we could ever satisfy; we need to spend our time based on a prioritized list. Next, you can begin to formulate your vision/mission but before you take that step, Step 3 will show us how to use our sub-conscious mind to create our future.

"Imagination is the beginning of creation. You imagine what you desire, you will what you imagine and at last you create what you will." - **George Bernard Shaw**

Step 3

SELF-ASSURED (CREATE YOUR COMPELLING FUTURE)

> *"My interest is in the future because I am going to spend the rest of my life there."* — Charles F. Kettering

We will explore various tools and techniques that will help us to create our future. The techniques build on developing a positive sense about who we are and where we want to go. Then, we can create in our minds eye, the future we want to have. We can accomplish this through positive visualization and affirmation.

STRATEGIZE FOR CHANGE

As you have been following along, you have developed a good understanding of who you are, what is important to you, and your personality type. You understand how and why you act under various conditions. Ideally, your beliefs are clearly in focus and you have a clear understanding of the priority each guiding principle has compared to the next. Now you can create your new reality!

First, you must decide what it is you want for your life. You must explore all the possibilities including your aspirations and dreams. Those possibilities are melded with your skills and abilities. Our self-vision is a major factor in what we accomplish. We need to be confident in our own development, skills, and successes. For us to see a positive future we must be confident about our capabilities. Now we can strategize about how to create a compelling future.

TRAINING THE SUBCONSCIOUS MIND

To achieve the results you are striving for, it will be necessary to write in your journal. It is known and understood that the process of writing your thoughts helps to reinforce what is in your mind. It also becomes a way to transfer those thoughts from your conscious to your subconscious. Your subconscious mind is a sleeping giant ready to support your every need. It works day and night for you; however, you must fill your subconscious mind with positively directed thoughts.

You must write out your desires clearly and use it to train your subconscious mind to see the result as a reality. You must give your mind orders repeatedly until with enough repetition, it believes your visualization as a new reality. The subconscious mind functions continuously. It will not remain idle. By doing this, you will convert your fantasies into creative imaginings and then to realities. This act of personal commitment will place the thoughts in your subconscious where it will be worked on continuously and enable the visions to become real.

Everything man creates first begins in his subconscious mind. We have a choice. We can allow negative thoughts to feed our subconscious or use positive thoughts that will lead us to success. You must provide your subconscious with positive input to act on and block out the negative thoughts. The choice is ours to make. We can be winners if we choose properly. If we fail to control our mind, we cannot control anything else. A positive state of mind cannot be purchased; we must create it, nurture it, and allow it to grow.

PROGRAM YOUR SUCCESS

Early in our childhood, we collect many impressions into our subconscious, ideas of ourselves as being good, bad, smart, stupid, etc. Over time, the impressions, which were inputted, collected, and imprinted into our subconscious, become the program controlling our self-image. Since our subconscious mind will prove our programming correct, i.e. if we establish "false" beliefs such as "I <u>can't</u> do that" then those beliefs will dictate the outcome; instead we are able to activate the positive response of "I can do it."

If we want to change our lives, we must provide our subconscious with positive self-images. Our subconscious cannot think for itself. It only produces results consistent with the image we placed there. We have the power to reprogram our deepest beliefs, control our thoughts, and change our lives to create successes. Each of us has the ability to program ourselves to perform in the manner we believe we are capable of achieving.

Success vs. Failure

In Psycho-Cybernetics, chapters Eight and Nine, Dr. Maltz defines two personality types using the acronyms *SUCCESS* and *FAILURE* as being comprised of the following:

S-ense of direction
U-nderstanding
C-ourage
C-harity
E-steem
S-elf-confidence
S-elf-acceptance

F-rustration
A-nger or aggressiveness
I-nsecurity
L-oneliness
U-ncertainty
R-esentment or rejection
E-mptiness

He defines the "success type" personality as someone who experiences the characteristics delineated by the success acronym. He describes the "failure type" personality as someone who experiences the traits delineated by the failure acronym. Dr. Maltz suggested that experiencing those characteristics should be used as symptoms of problems and reminders that a change is needed to move towards success. If you would like a more detailed explanation, I would recommend reading the books on Psycho-Cybernetics (see bibliography).

Achieve SUCCESS

Visualization is a key to achieving your success. You need to have those items in *SUCCESS*, such as, a sense of direction to know where you want to go. You must begin to see the path and understand why you are taking it. Your ability to visualize yourself having accomplished your goal and these actions will lead you to your success. You must see it, smell it, and totally visualize the event; draw your own mental picture. As Dr. Maltz said:

> *"...Fully 95 per cent of our behavior, feeling, and response is habitual...What we need to understand is that these habits, unlike addictions, can be modified, changed, or reversed, simply by taking the trouble to make a conscious decision-and then by practicing or "acting out" the new response or behavior."*

Success is a function of the amount of self-esteem you have. It is virtually impossible to achieve success without self-esteem. You build your success upon the foundation of self-esteem.

Learn from FAILURE

If we allow the *FAILURE* items to drive our lives, we will become failures. Therefore, when any of the failure mechanisms occur in our lives – and they will occur – we must replace them with the SUCCESS characteristics. Do not allow yourself to become stuck in the rut of failure. Failure and mediocrity are not states of being that you want to be in, nor do you want them to control you. Turn failures into something positive and learn from them.

There is no such thing as true failure; there are only results. Examine this example of a person who:

- Failed in business at age 21
- Was defeated in a legislative race at age 22
- Failed in business at age 24
- Sweetheart died at his age 26
- Had a nervous breakdown at age 27
- Lost a congressional race at age 34
- Lost a congressional race at age 36
- Lost a senatorial race at age 45
- Failed in an effort to become Vice President at age 47
- Lost a senatorial race at age 49
- Was elected president at age 52

Who was this person?

He was a person who did not allow those negative situations define him. He turned each event into a learning experience and tried to achieve success repeatedly. He bounced back from his adversities until he finally won the biggest prize. This was Abraham Lincoln, one of our greatest Presidents.

Another example of not allowing failure to stop us is this statement attributed to Thomas Alva Edison since he had so many failures before inventing the light bulb. He used failures as an opportunity to learn.

> *"...first found ten thousand ways not to invent the electric light bulb."*

Now analyze what happened in one of your recent negative experiences. Consider what you did and how you could handle that same situation better next time.

Self-Confidence

We must be prepared to overcome all negative influences and failures. Low self-image keeps us down and prevents us from succeeding. We become ensnared in the trap of believing our goals are not realistic but only fantasies. Our greatest deterrent to succeeding is a lack of self-confidence. We can overcome this handicap by repeating a series of positive acts that become burned into our subconscious until it is the path our neurons will follow. This cannot be just words that we believe either half-heartedly or not at all, but rather, it must be deeply felt and believed. We must "know" that we have the ability to achieve whatever is our goal. Spend time every day to re-enforce this and build your self-confidence by visualizing clearly and totally your accomplished goals. The next couple of sections entitled Positive Sensory Visualization and Affirmations provide more details.

Your thoughts can cause you to accomplish whatever you set your sights on. It is this power of autosuggestion that is described in the following poem:

> **"The Man Who Thinks He Can."**
> Walter D. Wintle, (1905)
>
> *If you think you are beaten, you are;*
> *If you think you dare not, you don't.*
> *If you'd like to win, but think you can't*
> *It's almost a cinch you won't.*
>
> *If you think you'll lose, you're lost.*
> *For out in the world we find*
> *Success begins with a fellow's will*
> *It's all in the state of mind.*
>
> *If you think you're outclassed, you are;*
> *You've got to think high to rise.*
> *You've got to be sure of yourself before*
> *You can ever win a prize.*
>
> *Life's battles don't always go*
> *To the stronger or faster man;*
> *But soon or late the man who wins*
> *Is the one WHO THINKS HE CAN.*

You can take steps to help you increase your self-confidence. Look at yourself in a mirror. See yourself smiling and smile whenever you are talking with people. Do not brag to others. Accept compliments graciously and say "Thank You" to anyone who pays you a compliment.

POSITIVE SENSORY VISUALIZATION

> *"See yourself and what you see you will become"* - **Aristotle**

> "The universe is change; *our life is what our thoughts make it."* - **Marcus Aurelius**

As you can infer from the quote, even going back to ancient Greece, successful people realized that outcomes are created in your mind before they are created physically. A winner has a dream that is more than a dream; it is a reality. They can totally visualize a burning passion. Visualization is a relaxation technique in which you create a mental image of the outcome you want to achieve. Once you visualize the outcome, your visualization includes not only seeing the achievement of your dream but all the facets around it. Imagine yourself succeeding in the steps leading up to the desired outcome. By doing so, you are mentally preparing to handle the event in real life.

Now make your vision of the future real by visualizing the accomplishment. Be as specific as you can about the situation. For example, if you thought about your ideal career position, your specificity would include items such as type of work, the industry it's in, the job title, geographic location, size of the organization, the degree of responsibility, the compensation package, and anything else to make this real to you.

People, who utilize positive sensory expectation, commit to the vision, talk about it in the present tense, believe in what they can achieve, and enjoy what they do. You can program your subconscious mind by providing positive self-talk. These positive affirmations will pass from your conscious mind to your subconscious mind. These affirmations are statements that you will write, read, and say to yourself with enthusiasm to convince your mind that it is the new operating instruction.

By writing your full-fledged positive sensory expectation, you make your visualization totally real and attainable. The purpose of writing the visualization helps to implant the details in your subconscious mind. The more precise your goal and detailed the situation surrounding it, the more ready you will be to attain your goals. You should write the details about the daily life you would have once the goal is realized.

Whatever you believe, with conviction, becomes your reality. Your conscious mind must see your goal accomplished. You must see, smell, and feel everything associated with your accomplished goal. As your belief becomes more intense, it will be transferred to your subconscious and become real. The more often you do this, the more likely it will become a habit and move into your subconscious. Remember, your mind cannot tell the difference between a real experience and one that the mind vividly imagines repeatedly.

ACTION ITEM 5: You can practice visualization in the minutes before you physically get up from your sleep. Simply close your eyes and breathe deeply. Picture yourself, after you have accomplished your goal, performing confidently and with ease. Make the visualization as real as possible. Hear the sounds, smell the fragrances, and see the colors. This practice of succeeding in your imagination will soon be your reality.

AFFIRMATIONS

In the introduction, we introduced the concept of positive programming of your subconscious. During our lives, we receive so much negative input to our subconscious by people telling us that we can't do this or that. The input is our negative programming. In addition, we begin to do our own negative self-talk so as to be destructive and in either case, it prevents us from achieving our desires.

You have the power to create whatever you want in your life. This power is within you and can be released through the practice of affirmations, which is a very effective method to overcome the negative programming by re-programming it. Begin to utilize positive affirmations to create new programming. One of the most important things you possess is your subconscious. Everything is possible if you properly program the subconscious. Affirmations are a powerful way of working with the subconscious to create what you desire.

When you recognize you are being negative, stop and question yourself. You will soon recognize that the negativity is incorrect and you can replace those inputs with positive affirmations. If it takes a bit more effort, clear that from your mind and pick up a piece of paper. Create a list of those things in life that you recognize as being good and give thanks for them. You may include whatever you have accomplished in life. This should free up those positive thoughts to help you to make positive affirmations and move forward towards your desires.

If you need more encouragement, read a good inspirational book. It can inspire you to dispel those negative thoughts and provide you with the motivation to move forward.

The steps in creating an affirmation begins with being certain it is in support of your guiding principles. If it goes against them, it will not work for you. The next key steps to consider as you create your affirmation are:

- Positive – State what you want, not what you don't want
- Self-Controlled – Begin with "I choose" as it is your choice and not what someone else wants you to do
- Present Tense – You want the subconscious to see the affirmation as if it's currently being achieved
- Specificity – See it happening in real time
- Intensity – The more deeply you feel about the affirmation, the more likely it will be achieved.
- Repetition – Keep making the affirmation for at least thirty days because you need time to program your subconscious properly.

The objective in using affirmations is to:
- release the negative program,
- program your subconscious with the positive program, and
- use repetition until you completely believe it.

You will read your clearly written goals, which we will develop in Step 5, and believe the words and picture depicted in your mind. You will need to follow your values, seek the cooperation of others, and perform actions that will cause others to believe in you. At least three times a day, you will say aloud your accomplished goals with the knowledge that it will be true. These steps will gradually influence your thoughts and actions.

Have you ever read about an Olympic athlete? Not only do they spend years physically training for their sport, they also practice visualizing the event. They spend a considerable amount of time visualizing the details of their event and their positive outcome. You will become successful if you emulate their approach. You will be a winner.

ACTION ITEM 6: Write your list of affirmations. It helps to use 3x5 index cards to record your affirmations and refer to them throughout the day. You can set aside a special time each day for your session. The two best times are either first thing in the morning or just prior to going to bed, whenever is convenient for you. If you choose the morning, you awaken refreshed; your mind is more receptive to positive thought patterns and better able to concentrate and receive new stimuli. This will also establish a positive mental attitude for the day ahead. The major benefit of the evening session is that your mind will continue your affirmation during your sleep. That is to say that the thought process established during your evening session will continue to operate on a subconscious level while you sleep. You choose which time period works for you; however, you need to make this a daily event.

> **AFFIRMATION WORKSHEET**
> Once you believe your thoughts create your reality, you can prepare your affirmations, which are the directions that you give to your subconscious mind to achieve your goal. Make the statement aloud 3-times in a row, 3-times a day for anyone to hear (best if done in front of a mirror).　　　　　　　　　　　　**Date:** __/____

Here are some tips for creating effective affirmations. Write affirmations:
1. in the present tense
2. in a positive statement (I am or I will, <u>not</u> I'll try)
3. within your control
4. short and easy to remember
5. in your speaking style
6. that are believable to yourself

Affirmation

By _____ I will _____
　　　Date　　　　　　　　　　　　　　　　Goal

_____

To reach my goal I will _____
　　　　　　　　　　　　　　　　　　Action

_____

_____

When I reach my goal I will _____
　　　　　　　Reward (This could be your why!)

_____

_____

_____

Your thoughts will create your reality!

The following poem, which is one of my personal favorites, summarizes the expected outcome of what this step is training you achieve. It is this attitude that you need to develop towards all that you want to do.

> *IT CAN BE DONE!*
>   Anon.
>
> *Somebody said that it couldn't be done,*
>   *But he, with a chuckle, replied*
> *That "maybe it couldn't," but he would be one*
>   *Who wouldn't say so till he'd tried.*
> *So he buckled right in, with a trace of a grin*
>   *On his face. If he worried, he hid it.*
> *He started to sing as he tackled the thing*
>   *That couldn't be done, and HE DID IT.*
>
> *Somebody scoffed: "Oh, you'll never do that;*
>   *At least no one ever has done it."*
> *But he took off his coat and he took off his hat,*
>   *And the first thing we knew he'd begun it,*
> *With the lift of his chin, and a bit of a grin,*
>   *Without any doubting or quiddit;*
> *He started to sing as he tackled the thing*
>   *That couldn't be done, and HE DID IT.*
>
> *There are thousands to tell you it can't be done;*
>   *There are thousands to prophesy failure;*
> *There are thousands to enumerate, one by one,*
>   *The dangers that wait to assail you;*
> *But just buckle in with a bit of a grin,*
>   *Then take off your coat and go to it;*
> *Just start in to sing as you tackle the thing*
>   *That "cannot be done,"*
> *And YOU'LL DO IT!*

The poem reinforces the concept of thinking positively and believing, the outcome will be positive, will result in success.

Elimination of negative thoughts and replacing them with positive attitude and visualization will enable accomplishment. I carry the poem with me and refer to it frequently. Believe in the power of positive thinking and perform accordingly and you will do it!

Step 4

VISION & MISSION (YOUR ASPIRATIONS & PURPOSE)

> *"Consider first the end."* –
> Leonardo da Vinci
> and
> *"Begin with the end in mind."* –
> Stephen Covey

You will create and document your vision and mission, that is, your sense of purpose or what is it you want to accomplish. Vision & Mission statements are complementary to each other and can be summarized as follows:

A *Vision statement* deals with the future and describes what, where, and who you want to become. It is an ideal that provides the framework, which will guide your choices that will determine the nature and direction of your future.

A *Mission statement* deals with the present and describes your fundamental purpose and plan of how to achieve your vision. It is the process to follow to get to your destination.

People occasionally mix the terms mission statement and vision statement and others use them interchangeably. We will use both and consider them complementary with vision representing your ideal future and mission describing your purpose and the process to achieve it. A vision without a mission will simply be a dream while having a vision with a mission will make the dream come true.

We will conclude this chapter on helping you to define your roles in life. When you clearly identify and concentrate on the important roles in your life, you can develop a vision for each role and develop a mission and goals associated with each role. You will take charge of your life and guide it in the direction you want to go.

YOUR MAJOR DEFINITE PURPOSE

Anyone recognized as being successful will know his or her "Major Definite Purpose". This is a term created by Napoleon Hill in his classic book on self-improvement "Think and Grow Rich." He associates being successful with having both a vision and mission. Then one can establish goals, focus effort, and achieve them. The positive action one takes will determine their "success".

Do not allow yourself to move aimlessly through life. It takes as much energy to wander as is needed to follow a clear path. The difference is knowing what your measure of success is and the path to take to get there. Successful people have a purpose to live for; they are cognizant of their "major definite purpose". The have a vision and mission. So let us begin by working this step of the process.

CREATE YOUR PERSONAL VISION

Everything happens for a reason. The hallmark of all high achievers is a burning why. They know what they want, how and when they will achieve it, but most importantly, they know WHY they want to become successful at achieving their goals. You won't become successful until and unless you identify, support, and empower your reasons why. Your why's provide fuel for achievement, and are the reasons behind all action and inaction. All things are created mentally before they are created physically. As quoted at the beginning of this Step, Covey defines this as "Begin with the End in Mind."

Think about who and what you want to be using what you have learned about yourself. Picture yourself in the best possible outcome. This is where you want to be very optimistic and reach out beyond what some may say is feasible. This stretch vision will open you up to ultimate possibilities. Even if you never accomplish it all, your accomplishments will outshine what would have happened without that vision.

> *"Imagination is more important than knowledge. For knowledge is limited to all we now know and understand, while imagination embraces the entire world."* - **Albert Einstein**

Use the techniques of Positive Sensory Visualization you learned in Step 3 to completely "see" your vision. A compelling vision will help you succeed way beyond where you would be without one. In business, the organizational vision answers the big question: "What is our business?" In personal planning, the question is "What is my life's business?" In both cases, the answer must define the reason for being. It is a description of what you want to become and what you want to accomplish.

You know and understand your strengths, weaknesses, character traits, and your desires. Now, put all the information together and your vision statement describes your desired outcome in detail. Close your eyes and envision a future with you being there and doing those things about which you dream. Include as many sensory details as you can. Envision the outcome achieved and see, feel, and smell everything around you. The more sensory details you provide, the more powerful the vision statement becomes. Describe the future; envision what it will be like and who will be there to share in everything with you. See the scene and hear the sounds.

Your Personal Vision Statement will provide a vehicle to focus your energies and efforts towards what you want to achieve. It defines your reason for being. There are a few key questions that you must ask and answer for yourself to help your vision to be clear and focused. They are:

1. What is the focus for your future? There are many options but you will need to focus your effort.

2. What is the scope of things you will or will not do? Review your guiding principles to help you in your determination. It is important to have established boundaries within which you will operate.

3. What are the key skills and capabilities required to make your vision happen? Knowing what you need will guide your efforts.

4. What are the steps in order to make everything happen? Having an idea of needing this before that makes it clear the path to follow.

5. What is required of you to make your vision happen? Once you know the previous answers, you can decide what is required of you.

Your vision statement should be simple enough to be clear yet articulated enough to provide a clear vision of your future. Take your time as the quality of your vision should stretch your expectations and aspirations and push your creativity. Also, successful people write down their vision statement on an index card or your PDA and read it aloud to themselves every day.

This activity helps to keep them focused on what and why they want to achieve their goals. Here are some examples of vision statements that were posted on the internet:

> "My vision is to be able to find a happy balance in my life; to gain back my health through dance and healthy food choices; I wish to be a successful mother, teacher, Christian, student, daughter, granddaughter, sister, employee, leader, and friend to all whom I have a duty to; to be a successful human being and a positive influence on others, through God's will; My goal is to enrich my life by improving my relationships with my family, friends, coworkers, and employers by using honesty, respectfulness, a positive attitude and always being aware of peoples' feelings and needs; to use my wisdom gained from my life experiences to help teen mothers, victims of domestic violence, and women everywhere to gain the empowerment they need in their lives through education and Christ; to never forget what I have been through for it gives me strength."

> "I am the spark that lights the fire. I aim to make a difference in someone's life, every day, in any way."

> "I am a house wife and also working, I want to balance my family and professional life - both. I want to become a successful human being. I want to improve my personality, and also the growth of the company and myself. I want to earn money to make my family and society happy."

> "My vision is to live life to its fullest. Organize my day to fill it with positive outlooks. Meet new people and make new life long friends. My true happiness lies in my future. My children are my life and have fulfilled it in many ways including three grandchildren. My horses are the stress reliever and I so enjoy riding and camping with friends and family. But there is an empty spot in my heart which I will have fulfilled, and when that is complete my life will be complete in every way I could imagine."

ACTION ITEM 7: Some people can quickly and simply describe their personal vision statement. If you are one of those people, document it and move on to the next topic. For most of us, it will be a process that is a bit more arduous. Find a quiet place where you will not be disturbed and begin the process of preparing a vision statement. Write down what it is you want for yourself without any limitations. Answer the following questions as thoroughly and completely as you can.

What are 3-5 things I really enjoy doing?

What makes me happy?

What can I do very well?

What would I do if I won the lottery? What would I stop doing?

What are my top 5 guiding principles?

What issues or causes do I care about very deeply?

With the answers to these questions available, it is time to pull it all together. Write out how you see yourself in the future. It should describe your hopes and dreams and evoke a sense of achievement. Use your skills at Positive Sensory Visualization and clearly describe what you want to be, do, own, be with, and feel. Remember that the purpose of your vision statement is to energize, motivate, and stimulate you. It may take several attempts to satisfy yourself that you have captured your vision of what you want to achieve. This is your written unique vision statement but it is not necessarily cast in stone and be rewritten whenever needed.

MY PERSONAL VISION STATEMENT

Imagine yourself in the future, include who you want to be, what you want to do, how you want to feel, who you have around you. **Date:** __/____

PERSONAL MISSION STATEMENT

Why or Purpose

Recall that in the second chapter of this book, we talked about Viktor Frankl, a psychiatrist and Nazi concentration camp survivor. He described his and other prisoners' experiences in the death camps as being stripped of everything, from all physical things to their own dignity. The survivors had a purpose for their existence and those who did not, died. The survivors had something they had yet to do. They had a mission.

A Personal Mission Statement is how you will express your Personal Vision in your daily life. It may be a few words or several pages, but it is not a "To-Do" list. It does reflect your uniqueness, supports your vision, and contains two basic elements. It addresses what you want to focus on - what you want to accomplish and what contributions you want to make. It describes specific ways you will accomplish your vision in your daily life and provides you with the overall direction as to how you intend to accomplish your vision.

The second is who you want to be - what character strengths you want to have, what qualities you want to develop, how you are going to live your life so as to achieve your vision, and clarifies your purpose and meaning. It is a declaration of who you are, why you exist, and what you will become.

It is okay to be where you are while heading somewhere else. In fact, the only place you can start is where you are right now. In addition, having a personal vision does not mean your life changes overnight. It is a gradual progression but it will change. Your personal mission statement provides the steps to get you there. A well-defined mission statement spells out your priorities so that you know what activities to say "Yes" to when you are making decisions about what actions to take.

Focus on the values and principles upon which your life's

activities are based, and describe what you want to be (your character), and do (your contributions and achievements). Review your activities from Step 1 and Step 2. Those results will help you to create your mission statement by providing the answers to the following questions:

Who am I?

What is important to me (VALUES)?

What am I good at & not so good at (SKILLS)?

What activities do I like or dislike (INTERESTS)?

What actions must I take to apply my Values and Vision?

We all have a purpose but many of us do not take the time to make it clear so our purpose must become our guiding light, much like a lighthouse sending out its beacon of light to guide the ships. As you work on developing your mission statement, you should examine your innermost thoughts and feelings to identify what is important to you. It will provide guidance for your day-to-day actions and decisions. You should refer and review it weekly to internalize it and make it into a living document.

When your mission is known, understood, accepted, and communicated, you can harness your energy and effort to make positive events happen. Like the ship in the lighthouse analogy, you know when you are headed in the correct direction and what to avoid as you accomplish your mission.

You need to invest time in this process. A mission statement is not something you do in one attempt. Also, it is not a sound-bite item. It takes careful analysis and introspection. Most likely, you will perform a number of rewrites to finalize it. This is a learning process and it changes as our experiences grow.

ACTION ITEM 8: Write your mission statement so that it explains how you are going to live your guiding principles and what actions you must take to achieve your personal vision. In order to write a personal mission statement that will provide direction and guidance for your life, you must be prepared to invest some serious time thinking about your personal mission. Don't rush into this effort. Ask yourself: What is it that you want in life? What force drives you to take action? Think about your values and desires.

Be specific and be clear in your words describing your mission. Define what you want: to be, to do, and to have. It does not have to be very long or overly complicated. It can be a few sentences. You will need to spend time thinking about and writing your mission statement. Your mission statement is not to impress anyone but rather written to inspire you to achieve your mission. If it seems difficult, write it down and come back to it later.

There is no specific formula to create your personal mission statement. The format is whatever is comfortable for you. Some helpful guidelines are:

- Write a mission statement to guide you in your day-to-day actions. It defines the how, that is, the specific way(s) you will accomplish your vision.
- Be clear on what you want and who you want to become.
- Keep it simple and brief.
- Make it positive.
- Identify your unique gifts and strategies.
- Identify what specific skills, qualities, and behaviors would be helpful to accomplish your mission.

For a simple approach to help to get you started, you can begin by filling in the blanks in the following:

My mission is to use my

_____

_____(skills, talents, etc.)
to

_____

_____(do what, actions, etc.) so
that

_____

_____(to accomplish what; a
result).

Allow a day to pass and go back to your mission statement and make adjustments to make it become real to you. Make sure it represents what you want and not anybody else. It should be motivating you and become your driving force.

Examples of what you may come up with are as follows:

> "I will live each day with faith, achievement, and adventure so that I could live my life with freedom, joy, and success. I am determined to graduate from a veterinarian college within 6 years, and then explore the world taking care of any animal in need."

> "I will look at situations from a positive light and remember that I could find myself in anyone's shoes. I value authenticity and joyfulness because seeing these traits in another makes me feel comfortable around them and know that I can trust them. I want to be one who others trust and feel comfortable with, so I will show my authentic, joyful self more often. To live each day with joyfulness and authenticity will allow me to be myself at the same time attract others who long to be their true selves. My positive outlook will bring me closer to friends, family members, co-workers, and send a ripple of positive energy into the world."

"To find happiness, fulfillment, and value in living I will CREATE the motivation needed by doing the following:

CONDUCT a life centered on the principles of excellence, growth, honesty, and fairness.

REMEMBER what is important in life is personal growth, family, health, respect, and sincerity.

EMULATE admirable characteristics in others, such as being enthusiastic, principle-centered, creative, patient, selfless, and committed.

APPRECIATE my strengths and develop talents as a person who is a communicator, intelligent, teacher, understanding, and imaginative.

TRAIN myself by acknowledging that I can be a procrastinator, disorganized, and vague and then by constantly striving to transform those weaknesses' into strengths.

ENVISION myself becoming a person who my:
- spouse thinks is industrious, self-reliant, and caring.
- child thinks is giving, principle-centered, and responsible.
- friend thinks is trustworthy, enthusiastic, and tolerant.
- associate thinks is balanced, patient, and trustworthy."

In order for it to become your driving force, your mission statement should be clear, concise, passionate, and positive. It will provide the necessary guidance for you to be able to develop your goals. It would be helpful if it is written on an index card and placed where you will see it every day. Read it aloud at least twice a day and it will become impressed upon your subconscious mind. It will become your driving force.

MY PERSONAL MISSION STATEMENT

Be clear in what you want and who you want to become. Identify what specific skills, qualities, and behaviors would be helpful to accomplish your mission.   **Date:** __/____

ROLES

While living our complex lives, we fill different roles. The role is a character assigned or assumed; a socially expected behavior pattern usually determined by an individual's status in a particular society. Allow me to restate this simply. We lead complex lives juggling roles as parent, child, employee, manager, student, teacher, or whatever, in multiple relationships that could defy a sense of balance.

Identify who is most important to you. Identify and examine your key roles in life to see that you provide guidance for all. For example, my roles are: husband, father, brother, Christian, associate, neighbor, change agent, and scholar. Be careful not to identify too many roles as the list may become too big to manage. Try to limit the list to the top 3 to 5 roles. Each role that you assume will need to be clarified as each has a different vision that will lead to setting goals to achieve in order to make your vision real.

For example, for my roles my vision could be:

Your Role	Your Vision for this Role
Husband	Since my spouse is the most important person in my life, I will endeavor to spend quality time with her providing comfort and support to ensure that we continue to contribute to and enjoy all the days of our life.
Father	I will spend some time each day speaking with my adult children and being involved in their individual lives. I enjoy their company, understand them, and provide to or receive from them much needed advice.
Brother	Keep in contact with my siblings, being sure to communicate my love and

	respect for them and to let them know that they are still a part of my life and that I am there for them.
Christian	Continue to learn about my faith, to treat everyone with the same kindness and love that my faith teaches, and to demonstrate the love of God.
Teacher	Deliver to others information that helps them to become better people and be able to live life their way.

ACTION ITEM 9: List your top 3 to 5 roles in life and write out your vision for each one. This effort will make it easier for you to set goals for each role that you fill. Here is a form "Roles I Live" that you can use to document your statements.

ROLES I LIVE	
Your Role	**Your Vision for this Role**

CREATE YOUR MIND MAP

So far, we have been mostly talking about linear, left-brain activities. Since many people accomplish more by utilizing visual aids, we are going to explore a non-linear, right-brain type activity. We can depict ourselves in a colorful drawing that incorporates our assessment of ourselves and our vision and mission. The picture may provide us with additional insight that we might not have gleaned from the words and paragraphs that we have completed thus far. AS the old saying goes "a picture is worth a thousand words."

Mind Mapping is a technique developed by Tony Buzan in the 1970's that utilizes pictures and words to improve and enhance your creative problem solving abilities and help you to "see" the solution or goal accomplishment in a non-linear fashion. Mind Maps depict not only facts, but also the overall structure of a topic and the relative importance of the individual parts. They help you to associate ideas and make connections that you might not have otherwise make. Mind Mapping enables you to identify and understand the structure of a topic and the way that the pieces of information fit together.

More importantly, Mind Maps provide a structure that enables creative problem solving, and they present information in a format that your mind will find easy to remember and analyze. This technique will enable you to see and understand how things in your life connect to everything else.

> *"A Mind Map® is a powerful graphic technique which provides a universal key to unlock the potential of the brain. It harnesses the full range of cortical skills - word, image, number, logic, rhythm, colour and spatial awareness - in a single, uniquely powerful manner. In so doing, it gives you the freedom to roam the infinite expanses of your brain."* — **Tony Buzan**

Once you know your purpose, priorities, and goals, you can

prepare a comprehensive picture looking at all the areas of your life. The key here is to brainstorm. It is to generate ideas and not necessarily in a linear or logical approach. You will be making connections that initially may not be obvious, by expanding your associations.

Your completed mind map may look like a tree diagram, a multi-armed octopus, or a work of art. Whatever the picture, you will be better able to see any disconnections or conflicts that will create problems and block the achievement of your goals and dreams. Take an hour a day for a couple of days to create your mind map.

The techniques utilized to create a Mind Map are as follows:

1. Start at the *center of the page in landscape orientation*, write the title of the subject you are exploring and draw a clear and strong visual image that depicts the general theme of the Mind Map.

2. Use just *key words* and/or whenever possible *images*. Enhance the drawing by using *colors* to depict themes or associations. Use visual aids to depict different elements.

3. As you come across major subdivisions or subheadings of the topic (or important facts that relate to the subject) draw lines out and create a sub-center. Label these lines with these subdivisions or subheadings. *Print* these words rather than writing in script as it will be easier to read and remember.

4. As you delve deeper into the subject and uncover another level of information (further subheadings, or individual facts) belonging to the subheadings above, draw these as lines linked to the subheading lines.

5. *Break boundaries and be creative.* Think three-dimensionally and do not limit yourself by the size of your paper, just add another sheet to the current drawing. Place ideas down as they occur and don't get stuck in one area, just move on to another area.

6. Utilize free association and do not be too quick to judge individual facts or ideas; just draw them.

7. Finally, have fun – use humor, exaggeration, or absurdity to make a point memorable.

Figure 1 & 2: Example of Mind Maps

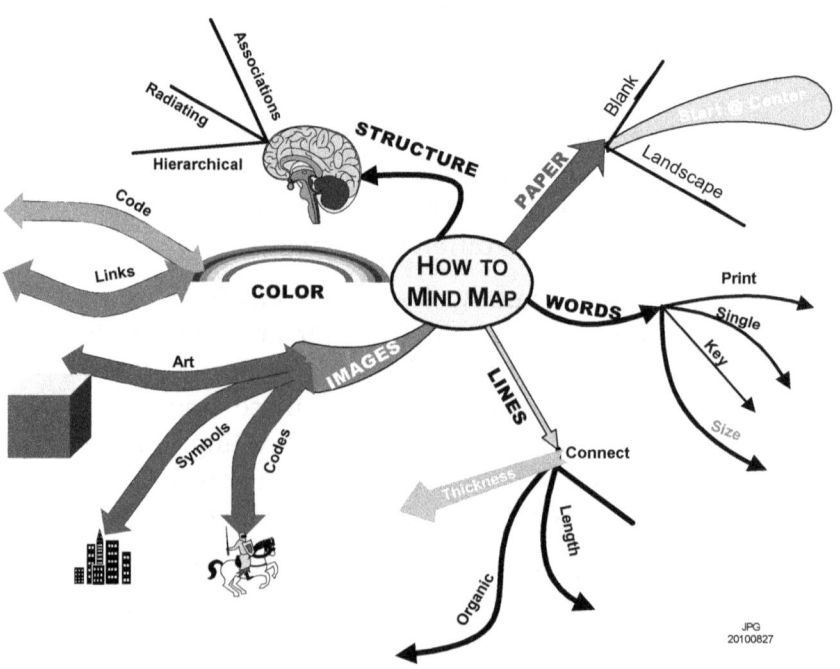

Mind Maps show not only facts, but also the overall structure of a subject and the relative importance of individual parts of it. They help you to associate ideas and make connections that you might not otherwise make. You can develop your own conventions to draw a Mind Map to make it effective for you. Some simple ideas are:

- Use single words or simple phrases
- Print rather than write
- Use symbols or images
- Use color to separate ideas

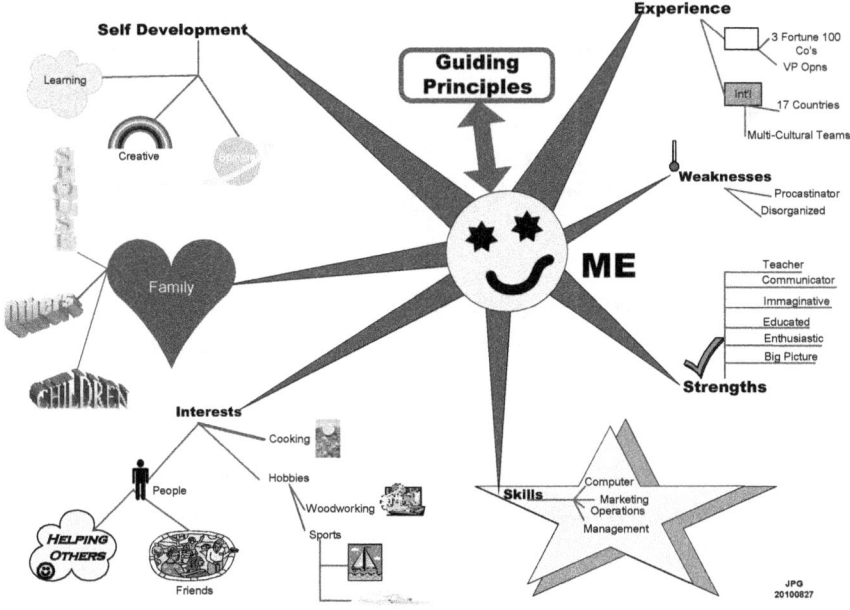

ACTION ITEM 10: Begin with a sheet of blank white paper and some colored pens or pencils. The larger the size of the paper the better. Draw a representative image of your guiding principles in the middle of the paper. Draw lines radiating out from your image(s) connecting to your desires. Continue to draw based on free association and try to answer the following questions"

> What do I want?
>
> Why do I want it?
>
> Why is it important to me?
>
> How will you accomplish it?

When you have generated all your ideas and answered the questions, look at your results. Organize the ideas into themes. Connect the ideas and look for more connections.

We will end the discussion of this step with an old poem that discusses the things to be desired.

> DESIDERATA
> (Written by Max Ehrmann in the 1920s, sometimes referred to as the Baltimore Prayer. The title is taken from the Latin meaning "things to be desired."
>
> Go placidly amid the noise and the haste, and remember what peace there may be in silence.
>
> As far as possible without surrender be on good terms with all persons. Speak your truth quietly and clearly; and listen to others, even to the dull and the ignorant; they too have their story.
>
> Avoid loud and aggressive persons; they are vexatious to the spirit.
>
> If you compare yourself with others, you may become vain or bitter, for always there will be greater and lesser persons than yourself. Enjoy your achievements as well as your plans.
>
> Keep interested in your own career, however humble; it is a real possession in the changing fortunes of time.

> Exercise caution in your business affairs, for the world is full of trickery. But let this not blind you to what virtue there is; many persons strive for high ideals, and everywhere life is full of heroism.
>
> Be yourself. Especially do not feign affection. Neither be cynical about love, for in the face of all aridity and disenchantment, it is as perennial as the grass.
>
> Take kindly the counsel of the years, gracefully surrendering the things of youth.
>
> Nurture strength of spirit to shield you in sudden misfortune. But do not distress yourself with dark imaginings. Many fears are born of fatigue and loneliness. Beyond a wholesome discipline, be gentle with yourself.
>
> You are a child of the universe no less than the trees and the stars; you have a right to be here.
>
> And whether or not it is clear to you, no doubt the universe is unfolding as it should.
>
> Therefore be at peace with God, whatever you conceive Him to be. And whatever your labors and aspirations, in the noisy confusion of life, keep peace in your soul. With all its sham, drudgery, and broken dreams, it is still a beautiful world.
>
> Be cheerful. Strive to be happy.

Most people's lives are difficult enough and filled with many distractions that makes it difficult to keep our thoughts and plans together. The written Guiding Principles, Vision, & Mission statements are beneficial tools to remind us of our purpose and plan of action. Writing the statements and having them readily available every day to refer to, keeps them fresh and in our daily thoughts. Also, do a mini-review regularly to determine how you are progressing and to see if any changes are in order.

> *"Twenty years from now you will be more disappointed by the things that you didn't do than by the ones you did do. So throw off the bowlines. Sail away from the safe harbor. Catch the trade winds in your sails. Explore. Dream. Discover."* – **Mark Twain**

Step 5

GOAL SETTING (DEVELOP THE PATH)

> *"If you don't know where you are going, any road will take you there."*
> — Lewis Carroll (1832 - 1898) Alice's Adventures in Wonderland

In Steps 2 and 4, we thought through what are our *Guiding Principles, Vision, Mission, & Roles*. This step explains how to ground your vision, mission, and purpose into well-conceived personal goals. It starts with your lifetime goals, and then goes through a series of lower level plans continuing in Step 6 to establish a daily "To-Do" list. By setting up this structure of plans, you can break down the biggest life goal into a number of easily manageable smaller tasks you need to do each day to achieve the lifetime goals.

Unfortunately, only a small percent of us set goals. It is this small group that are the achievers while the rest are like rudderless ships drifting aimlessly allowing external pressures to guide them. The effectiveness of goals can be seen in the incredible accomplishments of people such as Henry Ford who wanted to make cars affordable for everyone, Bill Gates whose goal was to have a computer in every household, and John F. Kennedy who set out to put a man on the moon within a decade. Remember – *the main reason people fail to achieve their goals is that they never set them in the first place.*

In order for us to change, we must learn to take charge of our future. Now that we know our destination, we must chart the path so that we may begin the journey. Goal setting is not magic but a skill that we can learn. It is a powerful process to concentrate our efforts and it provides needed motivation to make our vision a reality.

GOALS

A **goal** is the long-range, well-defined target or end toward which effort is directed. The goal statement provides clarity of the objective and gives direction, focus, and motivation.

Goal setting is a skill anyone can learn. The goal setting process is a standard technique that provides the bridge between long-term vision and short-term motivation. It helps us to determine our priorities, organize, make big decisions, and realize our dreams. The act of merely setting a goal brings about positive change for many people. When we set a goal, we are creating an exciting challenge for ourselves. Almost all motivational experts incorporate goal setting as an important part of their programs.

Goal setting is an extremely powerful technique for accomplishment used by athletes, successful business-people and achievers in all fields. It is a formal process for personal planning and builds on the earlier efforts of documenting your vision and mission. However, for goal setting to be effective, it requires more than just writing a list of dreams and filing it away. It requires that you invest time to be an active thinker and performer. You must approach this with some original thinking, lateral approaches, independence, and be prepared to assume responsibility for your actions. It focuses your efforts and helps you to organize your resources.

Goals are set on a number of different levels: Your guiding principles, vision and mission have been identified to help you to know what you want to do with your life and what large-scale goals you want to achieve. Now, break these down into smaller targets that you must achieve so that you reach your lifetime goals. Finally, once you have your targets, start working toward achieving them.

Now you will be working the steps towards turning your vision into your new reality. By setting goals on a routine basis, you decide what you want to achieve, and then move systematically towards the achievement of these goals. The process of setting goals and targets allows you to choose the path you will take in life. By knowing precisely what you want to achieve, you know what you have to concentrate on to accomplish it. In addition, as a corollary, you will know those items that are merely a distraction.

Sharp, clearly defined goals, enables you to focus your efforts, accomplish, measure and take pride in the achievement of those goals. You can see progress in what might previously have seemed to be a long pointless grind. By setting and achieving goals, you will also raise your self-confidence, as you recognize your ability and competence in attaining the goals that you have set. The process of completing goals and seeing this success gives you confidence that you will be able to achieve higher and more difficult goals.

Take time to think about what you would do if you knew you only had a very short time to live. Ask yourself "How would I spend my time if I only had "X" weeks to live? After you have thought through this concept, make plans to include these actions and activities into your daily life. We see the events that occur around us and in the world; you never know what may happen. Plan each day to live life to the fullest.

SETTING GOALS EFFECTIVELY

Well-formed Goal Statements

The Goal Statement forms the basis for the remainder of the process to achieve our vision so you should pay careful attention on formulating a clear and accurate goal statement. Set performance goals, not outcome goals. We must take care to set goals over which we have as much control as possible. There is nothing more frustrating than failing to achieve a personal goal for reasons beyond our control. These could be bad business environments, injury, or just bad luck. If we understand the fundamental nature of why we want what we want and we base our goals on personal performance, then we can have control over the achievement of our goals and draw satisfaction from them.

To set effective goals, each goal should be a positive statement and follow the broad guidelines below. A good way to remember how to define a goal statement is to utilize the SMART acronym used by many experts in goal setting. There are numerous variations as to what the acronym stands for, but we believe goals should be:

- Specific
- Measurable
- Attainable
- Relevant
- Time-specific

Specific

Set a specific goal, putting in WHAT you want to accomplish using action words, WHY you want to accomplish the goal with the specific reasons and the benefits of achieving the goal, and HOW are you going to achieve it. The Goal should be defined in specific detail so that we know exactly what we are trying to accomplish.

As previously described, our brains establish our success mechanism that will constantly be searching for ways to achieve our targets. According to Dr. Maltz, with clearly defined targets, our success mechanism, like the torpedo example, will be fully engaged and be adjusting to reach our targets and achieve the goal. If you do this, you will know exactly when you have achieved the goal, and can take complete satisfaction from having achieved it.

Measurable

Decide how you will measure your progress and completion of the goal. Establish specific criteria and milestones so you know exactly what you will accomplish and when it has been achieved. When you measure your progress, you stay on track. It helps you to see your progress and see how much further you still need to go. If you cannot measure it, you cannot manage it. Measure your progress and adjust as necessary to stay on track, and celebrate your accomplishment.

Attainable

It is important to know your capability as attainable is not a synonym for easy. Set goals that are practical and doable. They can be achieved within normal constraints and limited availability of resources. The objective should be one that you are willing and able to work towards; however, it may stretch your skills and knowledge.

All sorts of people (parents, media, and society) can set unrealistic goals for you. They will often do this in ignorance of your own desires and ambitions. Alternatively, only you can decide whether it is a high goal that is realistic or too high. Remember, if the goal is too difficult, you will set the stage for failure and if it is too easy, you may not consider it worth achieving. Build on your achievements but set your goals based on stretching your capabilities.

Relevant

Your statement of your goal to be accomplished should be relevant in a fashion declaring positive activity that focuses on actions you can take that are in your direct control and will produce results that helps you to achieve your mission and vision. Non-relevant goals are a waste of you time. Build on your achievements and set your goals based on achieving the next step towards your objectives.

Time-specific

Goals must have a deadline and the easiest way to do this is to establish start and completion dates. This will help in scheduling, monitoring, and appraising the status. Include dates, times and amounts for both the goal and sub-objectives so that you can measure achievement. Without a time limit, you will become prone to procrastination while with a deadline, you will have a sense of urgency and commitment that will move you towards the achievement of you goals.

CATEGORIES OF IMPORTANCE

Everyone has the same needs that must be addressed. In Step 1, you learned about Maslow's Hierarchy of Needs and in the section titled "Personal Inventory," we listed the three main categories and their sub-categories. How we address these needs and how detailed we get is profoundly personal. You have an opportunity to explore the possibilities for the important areas of your life.

To ensure your efforts will be very effective, you must actively confront and work on each area. You must address each important category and the associated needs to fulfill yourself and your dream. You should start with the 1-3 areas that if improved, would have the most *significant and immediate impact* on your life. In order to have a broad, balanced coverage of the important areas in your life, try to set goals in at least one area of each major category initially or preferably, all of the following categories, which are listed in the same order as discussed in Step 1.

Family:

How do you want your spouse or members of your extended family to see you? Do you want to be a parent? If so, what will you do to be a good parent? How are you going to care for your spouse, children, parents, and extended family?

Spiritual:

How will you achieve self-actualization? How will you go about exploring the meaning of life, understanding philosophy, morality, and mortality? How will you interact with nature, the arts, and religion? What kind of relationship would you like to have with God? How can you accomplish that relationship?

Education/Learning:

Is there any specific knowledge you want to acquire? How will you obtain it? What information and skills will you need to achieve your goals?

Financial:

How much do you want to earn by different periods in the future? How much money will you need to support your goals and priorities? How will you manage your resources to broaden your choices and options? You will need to be specific relative to your salary, budget, savings, debt, investments, etc.

Health & Well Being:

What can you do to manage your mental and physical health? How will you control your diet and exercise? What shape would you like to be in? Are there any athletic goals you want to achieve, or do you want good health deep into old age? How will you sustain your character development, sense of self-worth, temperament, stress level, integrity, etc? Is any part of your mindset holding you back? Is there any part of the way that you behave that upsets you? If so, set a goal to improve your behavior or find a solution to the problem. What kind of person would you like to be? What qualities will you have? What do you need to do to cultivate those qualities that you lack? What steps are you going to take to achieve these characteristics?

Home & Shelter:

Where do you want to live? What do you need and want for your personal space such as home, car, room, office, desk, etc? What do you have to do to maintain and improve the location(s) where you will live your life?

Career:

How will you earn a living? What would your ideal career be? What are your career goals? What are your interim goals? Do you need to have intermediate experiences to get you ready for the career you want? Choose a profession that you will enjoy, be successful, and be able to contribute to the well-being of others in one or more ways.

Social / Leisure:

How do you want to enjoy yourself? You should ensure that some of your life is for you! What are your interests, hobbies, or sources of entertainment? How do you want to vacation? What relationships are important to you?

Community Service:

How will you participate in community activities such as politics, volunteering, citizenship, etc.? Do you want to make the world a better place by your existence?

Behavior:

How do you plan to handle encountering and communicating with other kinds of people? How will you get along with them? How will you build a support system that will enable you to achieve your personal and professional goals?

OTHER FACTORS

In addition to setting goals effectively and addressing various areas of importance, other factors to keep in mind when setting your goals are:

Keep Goals Small

Keep the lower-level goals that you are trying to achieve small and attainable. If a goal is too large, then it may appear that you are not making progress towards it. Once you feel that you are not able to or cannot achieve your goal, you will get discouraged and may abandon the effort. By keeping goals small, the steps will be smaller thus providing more opportunities for achievement.

> *"The one who moves a mountain begins by carrying away small stones."* - **Confucius**

Equally as important, and as a balance to smaller goals, establish goals that are not too low. People tend to do this when they are afraid of failure or when they are lazy! You should set goals so that they are slightly out of your immediate grasp and provide some stretch, but not so far that there is no hope of achieving them. No one will put serious effort into achieving a goal that they believe is unrealistic. However, remember that your belief that a goal is unrealistic may be incorrect. If this could be the case, you can to change this belief by using imagery effectively.

Prioritize

As you establish your list of goals, too many can overwhelm you. You can shorten the list by prioritizing the goals from "A" (most important) to "C" (less important). Do not try too many categories, as that effort will add another level of complication. This approach helps to direct your attention to the most important goals. Limit the number of goals that you will focus on so as not to dilute your efforts and frustrate yourself.

Plan for Contingencies

Spend some time to identify the obstacles that you may face and plan on how to overcome them. Do not make this into a consuming event that prevents you from taking any action. You should know that some goals may not be attainable and you will need to adjust your goal or at least some steps to make the goal achievable.

Document Goals

Document your goals rather than keeping them in your head. Always state your goals as something positive to accomplish. Use your journal, which may be paper or electronic, and the forms provided to keep track of your journey.

The forms provided are useful to document the steps related to establishing and accomplishing your goals. The "Goal Sheet" provides a reminder of the various aspects of the conditions and requirements associated with each goal. The "Goals Table" provides a place to list your goals by priority and category. Do not forget the "My Personal Wins List" to set forth your list of accomplishments. Writing and reviewing the goals regularly, crystallizes them and provides more emphasis and force towards goal achievement.

ACTION ITEM 11: Gather up the documents or lists you have created thus far. Review the list of Desires, WOTS Up analysis, guiding principles, vision, mission, and roles. To help you to define specifically what you want, make a list of about 100 statements or questions that are important to fulfill your mission. Create this list at one sitting by writing quickly and making it a stream of consciousness. Don't worry about grammar, spelling, repeating the same question, or if it makes grammatical sense.

When you have finished, read your list and group them according to themes that are apparent but do not analyze nor judge them. Then consider the themes to see how your questions are grouped. Look at the groups and see if it leads you to see your goals that will get you to where you want to go. Choose goals that inspire you to reach out and accomplish them. They must be congruent with your major purpose in life and create a momentum that will pull you forward to your goal. In the following pages, we will go into detail about how to set goals. At that time, you can refine the goals that you have set for yourself.

In stating your goals, SHOULDs creates resistance while WANT's dissolve resistance. Do not forget to give power to your WANT's by adding BECAUSE plus the reasons for your choice. For example, "I WANT to go to night school to complete my degree BECAUSE I will be earning entry to my desired profession, making new friends, feeling great about my accomplishments, and improving my chances for future advancement." Use the Goal Sheet and Goals Table to begin to list your goals. Make sure your goals are in the categories we discussed. Also, be sure that the goals that you have set, are not what your parents, spouse, family, or employers want them to be, but instead be your goals.

Goal setting is an important method of:
- Deciding what is important for you to achieve in your life
- Separating what is important from what is irrelevant
- Motivating yourself to achievement
- Building your self-confidence based on measured achievement of goals

GOAL SHEET

Date _____ Goal Number _____ Sub-Goal Number _____

Target Achievement Date _____ Actual Achievement Date _____

Goal Category	Rank in Category	Overall Rank	Goal Category	Rank in Category	Overall Rank
Family			Home & Shelter		
Spiritual			Career		
Education/Learning			Social/Leisure		
Financial			Community Service		
Health & Well Being			Behavior		

Specific Goal: What exactly will you accomplish? How important is this goal to you? How are you going to achieve it?

Measurable: What are the specific criteria and milestones to know what you will accomplish and when?

Attainable: Is this goal achievable with effort and commitment? What skills will I have to use or acquire to achieve this goal? What resources do I currently have available that will help me to achieve my goal? What resources do I need to acquire? What other people do I need to obtain assistance from? What could possibly prevent you from achieving your goal? What actions do you need to change (break or adopt) to achieve the goal?

Relevant: Why is this goal significant? How does this goal help me to achieve my vision and/or mission? Provide specific reasons and benefits.

Time-specific: Establish start and completion dates.

Affirmation: What positive phrase will I use to establish a subconscious success mechanism?

Reward: How will I reward myself to celebrate my success?

Step 5 - Goal Setting

ACTION ITEM 12: Review the goals you set in the previous Action Item. Make sure your goals are in the categories we just discussed and assign a priority to them from A to C. Then review the goals and re-prioritize until you are satisfied that they reflect the shape of the life that you want to lead. Also, every time you complete a Goal Sheet, enter the goal in the Goals Table.

Example of a GOALS TABLE

Priority	#	Category	Goal	Time Frame	Measurement	Status A - Active C - Complete D - Dropped
A1		Family	Spend at least 10 hours per week with my family	Immediate	Time spent with family	C
A2		Career	Become the director of Human Resources	8 years	Achieving position of director	A
A3		Spiritual	Learn more about my religion	6 months	Being a more active participant at services	C
B1		Education	Earn my Bachelors' degree	Within 4 years	Bachelor's degree	C
B2		Financial	Have at least 6 months living expense saved	8 months	Money saved	C
C1		Leisure	Take a vacation in a warm climate	7 months	Having taken the vacation	A
C2		Social	Get more involved in the community	5 months	Join the Lions Club	D - Decided to do other

GOALS TABLE

Priority	#	Category	Goal	Time Frame	Measurement	Status A – Active C – Complete D – Dropped

GOAL ACHIEVEMENT

One of the key factors to success is goal achievement. You have learned how to set goals. Now you must stay focused and work towards achieving your goals. Once you achieve a goal, remember to celebrate your progress and note that each goal accomplished is a WIN for you. Keep track of your WINS using a sheet like the one following.

You have all the tools and knowledge to make choices to create significant changes in your life. Review your status regularly, add new goals, and make adjustments as needed.

MY PERSONAL WINS LIST		
Target Date	**Achieved**	**My Achievements**

"First comes thought; then organization of that thought, into ideas and plans; then transformation of those plans into reality." -
Napoleon Hill

Step 6

LIFE MANAGEMENT (PLAN THE WORK AND WORK THE PLAN)

> *"When it is obvious that the goals cannot be reached, don't adjust the goals, adjust the action steps."* - Confucius

Regardless of the language, it remains true that change is hard! This step brings together all of the previous work and helps you to prepare to apply the effort needed for the rest of your life. These steps are not a one-time look and see but rather part of a lifelong journey. Let us review the three points you developed and pursued to put you on your path. Up to now, you:

1. developed a clear *focus* and *inner clarity* about what is most important in your life.
2. created an unwavering and deep *passion*, driven by your subconscious mind that provided a spiritual sense of a greater purpose in your life.
3. kept a profound *commitment* to what you are doing every day.

These three items put you on your path but now you must manage your way with continuous actions.

PLAN THE WORK & WORK THE PLAN

Remember that change is hard work. It is always easier to continue to do what you are use to doing even when it is not good for you. It is always harder to introduce change. It takes extra hard work and attention to change oneself. Now that you have worked and developed various important piece-parts, you must have a plan to bring it all together in a useful way. There is an old saying *"if you fail to plan, you plan to fail."*

"TO-DO" Lists

Once we have a well-formed Goal Statement, we will need some direction to follow to achieve this Goal. We accomplish this by breaking down goals into manageable steps. For example, while the goal "Increase sales 25% by the end of the fiscal year without increasing advertising spending" may be a great goal statement, the goal is a monumental task without being broken down into smaller detailed steps. The creation of goal steps, more commonly known as To-Do's, provides us with an Action Plan when completed will lead to goal achievement. These steps also allow for tracking of progress towards the goal. Steps should be positive and not used to list obstacles that you must overcome. That approach focuses on the negative and negativity can kill motivation. Remember there IS power in positive thinking.

Create, use, and maintain a To-Do List to guide you towards goal attainment. Write down the tasks that face you. Most will

Step 6 – Life Management

be large so break them down into their component parts. If these parts still seem large, break them down again. Do this until you have listed everything that you have to do. The To-Do List contains all the tasks required to achieve your goals. It consolidates all the jobs that you have to do into one place. You can then prioritize these tasks into order of importance. This allows you to tackle the most important ones first.

Once you have done this, run through these jobs allocating priorities from A (very important) to C (unimportant). If too many tasks have a high priority, run through the list again and demote the less important ones. Once you have done this, rewrite the list in A B C order. Look through your "A's" and prioritize them. Repeat for the "B's" and put the "C's" aside. As you complete each task, mark it complete, and update the information to reflect what you actually did to accomplish the task if the effort was different from planned.

To-Do Lists are essential when you need to carry out a number of different tasks or different sorts of tasks, or when you have made a number of commitments. If you find that you missed something because you have forgotten to do it, then you need to keep a To-Do List. While To-Do Lists are very simple, they are also extremely powerful, both as a method of organizing yourself and as a way of reducing stress. Often problems may seem overwhelming or you may have a seemingly huge number of demands on your time. This may leave you feeling out of control, and overburdened with work.

You will then have a precise plan that you can use to eliminate the problems you face. You will be able to tackle these in order of importance. This allows you to separate important jobs from the many time-consuming trivial ones.

Different people use To-Do Lists in different ways in different situations. Some people motivate themselves by keeping their list relatively short and aim to complete it every day. Others keep one list and 'chip away' at it. It may be that you carry unimportant jobs from one To-Do List to the next. You may not be able to complete some very low priority jobs for several months. Only worry about this if you need to - if you are running up against a deadline for them, raise their priority.

If you have not used To-Do Lists before, try them now, as they are one of the keys to being really productive and efficient.

ACTION ITEM 13: Study your goals in your Goals Table and take each one and create smaller achievable tasks which we call To-Do's. Prioritize your To-Do List so that you will be more efficient working towards your goal. If you use prioritized To-Do Lists, you will ensure that:

- You tackle the most important jobs first, and do not waste time on trivial tasks.
- You remember to carry out all necessary tasks
- A large number of unimportant jobs do not stress you.

In order to draw up a prioritized To-Do list, you need to list all the tasks you must carry out. Mark the importance of the task next to it, with a priority from A (very important) to C (unimportant). Redraft the list into this order of importance.

"TO-DO" LIST		
\multicolumn{3}{|r|}{Date: __/____}		
PRIORITY	**ORDER**	**ITEM**

Now carry out the jobs at the top of the list first. These are the most important, most beneficial tasks to complete.

Time Management

It is essential to utilize the fundamental principles of time management. You must learn to take control over your day. Provide time each day to review, plan, and contemplate. Of course, you should have some flexibility built into your day to account for the unexpected. Time management is critical to your schedule. A rule of thumb is to schedule 80% of your time and leave 20% for the unplanned things that come up. For example, set up a routine of awaking at a set time each day, early enough to fit in and spend time to plan that day or before you retire for the evening and plan the next days' activities.

This effort provides you with guidance for that day and greatly reduces the unpredictability. Also, it gives you control of your time and your actions since your goals are refreshed and right in front of you. You procrastinate when you allow factors such as interest level, fear, laziness, etc. to deter you from placing your energies where they belong. You must apply self-discipline especially since you have the final responsibility to establish the goals, prioritize timing, and amount of effort applied.

Have you ever heard of Pareto's Law? It can be expressed as 80% of the results come from 20% of the effort. If you examine what you have been doing lately, it should become obvious that 80% of your time was spent in doing things that were not very useful or productive and conversely, 20% of your effort was spent to generate 80% of the positive results. The ratio may not be precise but it usually holds true and frequently it can be even more skewed than 80:20. Discover the things you do that are inefficient and eliminate them. Focus on those things that bring the greatest results.

In all parts of your life, you must make effective use of time. By being inefficient, you affect everything & everyone in your sphere of influence. By becoming more organized, you can identify what is important to you, establish a list of priorities, and spend quality/effective time in each area of your life. You must be in control of what you do and when you do it, rather than being adrift and allowing the shifting winds to move you about. You must recognize that you cannot control the winds. However, you will be better prepared to use them to your advantage and to assist in your accomplishments.

One approach is to keep a daily agenda and enter everything that you do. Update it as you accomplish items on the list, including time. Record the duration and with whom you spoke or met for every phone call and meeting. You will have a complete record of everything you did each day. Within a few days, you will have enough data to see where and how you spend your time. You will be in a position to convert wasted time into productive time. It will enable you to focus on doing things that will move you towards accomplishing your goals. Record your daily accomplishments in your journal, as it will keep you on-track towards achieving your goals.

Schedule

Both Charles R. Hobbs and Stephen Covey present the concept of a matrix that depicts the relationship of urgency and importance. Everyone recognizes the need to work on tasks that are both urgent and important. By definition urgent tasks should be completed immediately. That would indicate we definitely must work on activities in Quadrant 1 but we should not become slaves to urgent tasks.

	URGENT	NOT URGENT
IMPORTANT	**Q1** NECESSARY	**Q2** PERSONAL LEADERSHIP Planning Preparation Prevention
NOT IMPORTANT	**Q3** DECEPTIVE	**Q4** FEEL GOOD & WASTE

We have become programmed to respond to the urgent, such as

the ringing telephone. For most of us, the ring of a telephone causes us to drop whatever we are doing and answer the telephone. We react to the ring of a telephone just like Pavlov's dogs, which were trained to salivate when a bell rang, food or no food. Now with cellular telephones, it has become an even more acute problem. We need to decide how we want to deal with the ringing phone. For example, when I used to have meetings in my office, I decided that the meeting took precedence over the ringing phone. Therefore, if my phone rang, it went unanswered until after the meeting was over. It took a while before I became comfortable with ignoring a ringing telephone in my office but it surely made a difference in the productivity of my meetings.

It is Quadrant 2, which is the congruence of important and not urgent, which most of us tend to neglect, that we must focus on. It is here that the greatest payoff comes. By working these activities, we will position ourselves to complete important tasks and prevent crises.

When we need to make the time for Quadrant 2, it is obvious that we will utilize the time from Quadrant 4 efforts but the important thing is to realize that Quadrant 3 activities are deceptive. It is here where activities are urgent but not important. You must realize that time management and urgency are not synonymous concepts with importance and implement some judicious decisions on which Q3 activities you will spend time in doing and whether or not to delegate some of those activities.

Efficacy

Effectiveness is a measure of the positive results obtained or how worthwhile is the thing we choose to do. Efficiency is doing something with the least amount of effort, time, and resources. Notice that either of the two can be performed without regard for the other, that is, your efforts can be effective but not efficient or visa-versa.

We will utilize an approach that combines both effectiveness and efficiency. The term for the combined effect is efficacy, that is, the power to produce the desired result or effect both effectively and efficiently. This process is the putting together of the necessary To-Dos to enable you to accomplish more of the right things faster and easier.

ACTION ITEM 14: Think about and discuss why we work on quadrant 1 activities and the absolute need to work on Quadrant 2 activities, even at the expense of Quadrant 3 and 4 activities. Look at your activities and place them in the appropriate quadrant. For each of the Quadrant 1 & 3 activities, ask yourself "What can I do to prevent this activity from reoccurring or at least from it having such urgency?" Answering this question should help you to identify Quadrant 2 activities that you should be doing. Once you identify these activities, schedule and implement them.

Yogi Berra, the famous New York Yankee baseball player and manager, known for his remarks that are both provocative and simple, had this to say:

> "If you don't know where you are going, you will wind up somewhere else."

Develop the details of your plan and provide for contingent actions if the situation is not as you envisaged. The contingency plan provides for specific actions to be taken when an event or condition that was not planned for actually takes place. The advantage of developing a contingency plan is that it makes us look at dimensions in the environment other than probable events. It deals with the "What if?" situation. It prepares us to manage through those events which we can't control. Now prepare an overall schedule of your time that contains the following action items:

Daily
Choose a time of day to set aside at least 15 to 30 minutes to

review your daily To-Do list. Most people find it best to do this either, at the end of each day or preferably first thing in the morning. Do whichever works best for you but more importantly, stick to your schedule. It is important to allocate this time but be flexible. If an unexpected event occurs, simply re-schedule your quiet time. Remember successful people do whatever it takes to succeed! Use this time to:

a) consider what is positive about this day,
b) think about taking care of your responsibilities and still have some fun,
c) ponder your goals (A1, A2, etc.), and
d) plan the day's activities.

There will be those days when unexpected events will keep you from accomplishing one or more of your tasks. Re-schedule as soon as possible

Weekly
Review your goals and mark off those you have completed during the past week. Add any new goals for the coming week. Measure your progress towards accomplishing each goal. By focusing on each week at a time, you can avoid being overwhelmed by all there is to accomplish to achieve your goal. Make sure you have established your daily To-Do lists.

Monthly
Review your progress towards achieving your goals. Make sure the goals align with your guiding principles and mission statement. Adjust the goal or measurement, as necessary. Create milestones in your calendar as a reminder of the goal you are working to accomplish to help you stay focused. Without a clear goal, we will always be distracted and spend our energy on secondary things. Martin Luther King told people "Keep your eye on the prize." If you follow his advice, you will have successes. Review your successes and celebrate them.

Quarterly or Half-Yearly
Review and re-evaluate all your Guiding Principles, Vision and

Mission Statements, and Roles. Re-evaluate your mission statement and adjust or change it where necessary. This will enable you to fine-tune your life. Make sure your goals are clearly defined and measurable. Break your larger goals into smaller goals that are more manageable. Track your progress towards achieving each goal.

ACTION ITEM 15: Set aside two hours to gather up and think through your lifetime goals in each of the categories. This will include those roles that you have or want to play. Establish long-term objectives, intermediate objectives, and short-term goals. Think about a plan to fulfill your goals, including a 5-year plan, 1-year plan, 6-month plan, and a 1-month plan.

. For example, "I will work with my personal calendar and spend more time planning. Each morning, I will spend a minimum of 1/2 hour to plan my activities for that day." The plan is a necessary step in your effort to create change, but it is not sufficient to create the change you desire. You have to work the plan before you will see some progress.

Put your plan into action. Keep focused on the To-Do's or the smaller steps that you can accomplish and the larger goal will happen. Tomorrow, do those jobs and start to use goal setting routinely!

Be prepared to modify your plan as needed. While you have created a plan, and that is what it is – a plan, events and/or problems will arise that you did not anticipate. Edit and change your plan to make it better and workable. The editing process will occur as many times as needed until you achieve your goal.

You should allow yourself to enjoy the achievement of goals and reward yourself appropriately. Draw lessons where appropriate, and feed these back into future performance.

STEP	ACTION
	WEEKLY REVIEW Date: __/____
1	Review / Edit Mission & Vision
2	Review last week ➤ What goals were achieved? ➤ What were the challenges? ➤ What progress have you made towards accomplishing your goals?
3	Decide which Roles to act on this week
4	Decide which category Goals to work on this week
5	Establish your daily TO-DO items to concentrate on during the coming week

Procrastination

Procrastination is so easy and each of us has been guilty of it at one time or another. Procrastination usually is a result of one of two things. One reason is that we fear what we have to do and often it is because it is something we are not good at doing. If that is the reason for the procrastination, we have a few choices. We can try to get someone else to do it for us, we can pique our interest enough to learn how to do the task so it will not be as distasteful, or we can face the situation and do the task. Any of the solutions properly applied makes the procrastination disappear.

The other reason is that the task is very complex so that we are overwhelmed and thus paralyzed by the very thought of it. The solution for this situation either is to break the task into more manageable pieces in less complex steps or in shorter periods until the whole task is completed.

> *"Even if you are on the right track, you will get run over if you just sit there."* - **Will Rogers**

We must apply self-discipline especially since we have the final responsibility to establish the goals, priorities, timing, and amount of effort applied. People who are winners concentrate on their main goals. They do not procrastinate or allow themselves to be sidetracked. You must work on the items that are important and not allow those items to sit aside until the last minute. Commit yourself to start and the task will be on its way and it will gain momentum.

When you are preoccupied, your attention is engaged in something other than the pertinent happenings around you. It is irrelevant thought and action.

> *"Any moment you are preoccupied is a moment you are not free to manage your time. You can steadily win back control of events as you win back attention from preoccupation."* - **James McKay**

When you have achieved a goal, take the time to enjoy the satisfaction of having done so. Celebrate! Absorb the implications of the goal achievement, and observe the progress you have made towards other goals. If the goal was a significant one, reward yourself appropriately. With the experience of having achieved this goal, review the rest of your goal plans:

- If you achieved the goal too easily, make your next goals harder

- If the goal took a dispiriting length of time to achieve, make the next goals a little easier
- If you learned something that would lead you to change other goals, do so
- If while achieving the goal you noticed a deficit in your skills, decide whether to set goals to fix this.

Keep Moving

In addition to avoiding procrastination, winners are highly motivated, work hard, and keep moving towards achieving their goals. They have a burning desire to succeed and are willing to do whatever it takes to achieve success. You cannot just sit around and expect everything to come to you. Failure to meet goals generally is not that important as long as you learn from the experience and feed the lessons learned back into your goal-setting process. Keep moving and work your To-Do's.

DECISION MAKING & RISK TAKING (DECISION IS A RISK ROOTED IN COURAGE)

Having clearly identified and written your guiding principles, decisions are made easier. When faced with a decision, think about how the choice you will make is in line with your guiding principles. When your actions are in accord with your guiding principles, the decisions become easy. Once principles and long-range goals are written, refined, and prioritized, ask yourself "What more specifically must I do to cause each goal to happen?"

If you have difficulty in making an important decision, most likely, it is a function of you being unclear about your guiding principles.

> "You can increase your output as you increase your capacity to get accurate, clear, fast impressions of what is going on around you." – **James McKay**

Everything that happens in your life begins with a decision. It is in these moments of decision that your destiny is shaped. The decisions, that you are making every day, shapes who you are and what you will become. Your decisions should be such as to lead you towards your goals. Use your decision-making abilities to get past any excuses. It can change your relationships, your working environment, and your whole life.

IF YOU DECIDE TO, YOU CAN DO ANYTHING.

Concentrate Your Efforts

You need to become the conductor who is leading your life's orchestra. As you move forward, you need to be continually aware of what it is you really want. Keep asking that of yourself and answer it honestly. It will clear the way for you.

Changing your behavior takes time, so do not rush the process. You must keep on top of your efforts until the behavior change becomes permanent.

Do not wait for the motivation to arrive. You must initiate the action and follow through with it. You will become energized to accomplish your personal goals.

Effective Decision Making

Decision making is a process that leads to the selection of a course of action among several alternatives. The phrase "making a decision" implies that there are a number of alternatives to be considered, thus we want not only to identify as many of these alternatives as possible but to choose the one that

- has the highest probability of success or effectiveness, and
- best fits with our goals, desires, lifestyle, values, etc.

The process could be rational or irrational, logical or illogical, emotional or not, and analytical or not. In addition, very few decisions are made with absolute certainty because complete knowledge about all the alternatives is seldom possible. Thus, every decision involves a certain amount of risk.

To be effective, one should follow the following process:
1. Define the problem – Seek to understand more about why you think there is a problem.
    a. Observe and learn to be more aware of yourself, your actions, the situation, and people around you.
    b. Concentrate your energy; especially focus your mental energy on what is most important to you.
    c. Perceive and become intensely aware and truly experience the situation.
    d. Recall similar situations and remember both the "good" and the "bad" to avoid selective recall.
    e. Document the problem.
2. Assess Implications – Analyze the problem, and how it affects you.
3. Explore options – Use varying techniques such as brainstorming, Pareto analysis, etc.
4. Define outcome wanted – Define what is important and what it is that you would prefer the outcome to be.
5. Weigh Pros and Cons – Anticipate the consequences of a decision. Experiment and test with others whenever possible.
6. Decide and Act – After having completed the decision making process, choose those actions consistent with your values that will enable you to achieve your goals.

Taking Risks

Any achievement results from taking some risk in order to make something happen. Sometimes the result is not what you expected. Recognize that you made a mistake and do not spend time blaming others, instead learn from the experience, change your course of action, and move on. Understand that this risk did not work out. Overall, you will take some risks and most of them will work out for you.

Goal Adjustments

Remember too that your goals will change as you mature. Adjust them regularly to reflect this growth in your personality. If goals do not hold any attraction any longer, then let them go. Goal setting is your servant, not your master. It should bring you real pleasure, satisfaction and a sense of achievement.

ACTION ITEM 16: Choose an issue that has been a problem for you. Apply the six-step process discussed and work the issue. You should be able to resolve the issue and put it away.

SUPPORT TEAMS (HELP IS THERE FOR YOU)

Most of us realize that we could learn from the experiences of other people. There was a time when people served an apprenticeship for up to seven years in order to learn from a master. Experience and modern behavioral science has demonstrated that people learn best from observing others and modeling their behavior after someone else who has demonstrated their abilities. People who choose to model the attitude, behavior, and characteristics of someone who is successful, become successful themselves. Since apprenticing is not the normal occurrence today, you must choose some fresh methods to learn from others, such as mentors and role models to emulate and a team to support your efforts.

One of the benefits of working with other people is to have someone to emulate. The learning process relies upon good communication and you must assume your share of the responsibility. Good communication requires both talking succinctly and listening intently. People will share with you what they know, how they do things, and what they are thinking when performing the activity. These are your greatest resource. In time, you will find people who will offer you encouragement, support, and help and you need to build and maintain your relationships with them. They are people who are your real friends and want to see you succeed.

Team

There was a time when immigrants came to this country and formed alliances. These ethnic groups worked together to help one another to accomplish their goals; frequently they pooled their money to start a business. In turn, each person in the alliance was helped. Today, one can do something similar by working with a few close people whom you feel will understand what it is you are working towards can provide the necessary support. These people could include your spouse, friend, business associate, etc. It is important these people be supportive and provide you with positive reinforcement. You can either work together on the same goal or support one another so each can work on their individual goal. This approach works when there are written objectives and regularly scheduled meetings to discuss what is happening, resolving issues, and motivating each other.

Napoleon Hill speaks of the "Mastermind Alliance" which is built on the cooperation of two or more people who help one another for accomplishing a given task. A direct result of this association is an effect of increased mental power that is available to anyone in the group. This can be observed in various groups of minds working towards a common cause, such as musicians, sports teams, religious groups, etc.

Hill tells us that the key to a mastermind alliance is in the harmony and allegiance they have to one another. The team can ideally consist of about 5 people who are brought together. Before you try to gather the team, you should adopt a major definite purpose or mission. Then you can carefully choose people who will help you to achieve your goal. The individuals must be able to work harmoniously. Establish a time and place for regular meetings, generally once a week for about an hour.

Mentors

As we go through life, most people come across mentors such as parents, teachers, associates, etc. that have had an impact upon their life. Sometimes, it could be an experienced businessperson who will work one-on-one with you to teach you and provide step-by-step guidance to improve your business processes, skills, knowledge, and relationships.

Find someone who has accomplished goals that are similar to yours. It should be someone who can provide the time and energy to help you to achieve your goals; someone who has similar values to you and who will be willing to provide guidance that you will listen to.

Role Models

Role Models are people from whom we can study and learn from their behaviors and actions. They can be anyone who can provide you with examples of how to accomplish things easier, better, faster, etc. It is a great help to us to have role models to emulate. It is important to choose the right role models. Choose people who can help you not people who entertain you or make you feel good. You want to find people that have something to give to you; a trait, technique, approach, etc.

There is much written about leaders and important people from all walks of life. You can ingest a tremendous amount of information about what, why, and how these people accomplish their activities and emulate those behaviors in your own life. However, don't restrict yourself because a role model can be anyone around you who can teach you something directly or indirectly. Look at people around you who are accomplishing more or are more "successful" than you.

Positive Models

Study people who have accomplished things for themselves and model their actions and behaviors. Find people who have made lasting changes. Find out what they did as an alternative to their old "bad" behavior. Find someone who has been able to overcome their negative actions that are similar to those you want to change.

Find someone who is living the life you want to have. This person may be the role model who can and will provide you with some answers. The way to expand our lives is to model the lives of those who are succeeding with their life. As you meet these people, ask them questions such as, "In your opinion, what makes you different? What beliefs do you have that separates you from the others?

Helen Keller is a great role model. She was deaf, dumb, and blind. (Note that in this context, dumb means lacking speech not that she was stupid.) Despite her handicaps, she was taught how to communicate and became a person who accomplished much. She is clear evidence that if one sets their mind to accomplishing something; they can accomplish their goals if they do not accept defeat as a way of life. No one will be defeated unless they accept defeat as a reality.

> *"WE ARE WHAT WE THINK. All that we are arises from our thoughts. With our thoughts we make the world."* – **Buddha**

Art Linkletter continued to travel about 150,000 miles a year to speak and write books until his death at age ninety-seven. In his last book, he discussed many of the points raised in this book as what to do to continue to be vital and alive as one becomes older. He discusses the way to develop the right mind-set and ways to make "smart, brave choices about your future." He labels these as "The Ten Empowerments." The ten principles are:

1. You can defy the stereotypes of old age.
2. You can determine your longevity.
3. You can make new friends and create rich new relationships.
4. You can be financially secure as long as you live.
5. You can be more fit than you were at thirty.

6. You can keep your mind agile and sharp.
7. You can make a positive difference in the world.
8. You can discover and nurture your creativity.
9. You can look forward, not back.
10. You can create a life filled with new experiences, inspiration, and great achievements.

There is so much to learn from Art Linkletter. You can study his life or follow his example. Reading his book "How to Make the Rest of Your Life the Best of Your Life" which he co-authored with Mark Victor Hansen, will provide insights to his principles and how he lives those principles.

Negative Models

People can learn from their own mistakes. However, to become more efficient, you can also learn from the mistakes of others. Take the time to study these "negative" role models to learn what mistakes they made and you would want to avoid. You can learn different approaches to overcoming challenges and select which ones work for you. Use what you learned about yourself in Step 1 to determine which styles fit your personality.

You can choose people from modern times or from the past. The important thing is to look at their mistakes and choose not to make those same mistakes in your life. Turn their negative experience into a positive learning experience for you. Remember, learning what not to do can be as important as learning what to do.

ACTION ITEM 17: Make a list of 5 of the most important people in your life. Schedule a meeting with them and spend time to continue your relationship with them. Next, create a list of 5 people you either currently know or would like to meet so that you can know better and learn from. Think about what specific information you would like to know about them or learn from them. Set up a meeting with them.

PERSERVERANCE (THE TOUGH GETS GOING WHEN THE GOING GETS TOUGH)

> *"Nothing in the world can take the place of persistence.*
> *Talent will not; nothing is more common than unsuccessful men with talent.*
> *Education will not; the world is full of educated derelicts.*
> *Persistence and determination alone are omnipotent."*
> **– Calvin Coolidge**

Motivation, Commitment and Habit

Motivation and commitment are what make us strive to achieve. They give us the push, desire, and resolve to complete all of the other steps in the goal process. This motivation can be obtained by developing a personal statement that creates a high level of emotion and energy that guarantees achievement. One self-help expert said that as a child he was kicked out of his local country club pool because he was not a member. In response he made a goal that he would one day have a pool that is one foot bigger than that country club's pool. The incident provided the necessary motivation for him to achieve this goal.

Winners are motivated people. Without motivation, your performance will suffer but with motivation and commitment, you will achieve your desired objectives. You will learn how to become a top performer and accomplish all that is important to you. Remember, winners do things that get the results while others do things that are pleasing to them. One needs both motivation and commitment to take the necessary actions to achieve their objectives.

The whole world steps aside when a committed person passes. Such is the power of deciding to follow through. Determination brings freedom and control. Commitment enables us to continue on without stopping. Thomas Edison invented the electric lamp.

He worked on the design for years and had thousands of failed designs before he finally succeeded. He stood by his dream until he made it work. What do you think we would be using for light had he quit? The world is filled with opportunities for people who do not quit – those who continue to have a commitment.

It is also called DETERMINATION. Commitment means NO MATTER WHAT! And determination is a refusal to allow obstacles to stop us. Here is how two people expressed this idea:

> *"The difference between a successful person and others is not a lack of strength, not a lack of knowledge, but rather in a lack of WILL."* - **Vince Lombardi** (1913 ~ 1970)

> *"People do not lack strength; they lack WILL."* – **Victor Hugo** (1802 ~ 1885)

In both cases, the word 'WILL' refers to commitment or determination.

Motivation and commitment are specific to the situation and only we can form statements that will ensure we reach our goal quickly. Commitment creates more accountability and is what sets us on direct course to reach our goals. It may create costly negative consequences upon failure to attain a goal. The more personal we make our motivation and commitment statements for each goal; the more motivated we will be to accomplish our goal. The following poem provides some real insight into the power of commitment.

> **The Power of Commitment**
>
> Ed Hirsch
>
> *It makes your knees shake, it makes your stomach tight, it makes you calm with relief.*
> *It can determine the way you feel and the way you act.*
> *It's what creates business relationships and also what can destroy them.*
> *It's something we succeed at one minute and fail at the next.*
> *It distinguishes doers from dreamers, champions from wanna-be's.*
> *It sorts our confusion, clarifies the mysterious and has the ability to dramatically impact your business.*
> *It can alter the quality of your life, the extent of your achievements, and the measure of your success.*
> *It has the power to create what is possible.*
> **It's called COMMITMENT!**

We must make the correct actions into good habits. A habit is formed by doing an action repeatedly, and good habits are formed by doing the correct action repeatedly. The experts have said that it takes at least 21 days to make or break a habit. With a written goal, the use of positive sensory visualization and positive affirmations, you will develop the motivation and commitment to change and have a new, positive habit. Although you may have seen the poem following, read and contemplate it as it provides some needed insight to habit.

> ### *The Power of Habit*
> Ed Hirsch
>
> *I am your constant companion.*
> *I am your greatest helper or your heaviest burden.*
> *I will push you onward or drag you down to failure.*
> *I am completely at your command.*
> *Half the things you do, you might just as well turn over to me,*
> *And I will be able to do them quickly and correctly.*
> *I am easily managed; you must merely be firm with me.*
> *Show me exactly how you want something done,*
> *And after a few lessons I will do it automatically.*
> *I am the servant of all great individuals.*
> *And, alas, of all failures as well.*
> *Those who are great, I have made great.*
> *Those who are failures, I have made failures.*
> *I am not a machine, though I work with all the precision of a machine.*
> *Plus, the intelligence of a human being.*
> *You may run me for profit, or run me for ruin;*
> *It makes no difference to me.*
> *Take me, train me, be firm with me*
> *And I will put the world at your feet.*
> *Be easy with me, and I will destroy you.*
> *Who am I?*
> **I am HABIT!**

Reminders and Keeping on Track

Reaching your goals requires perseverance and regular attention. You must have some sort of system to keep you reminded and accountable. As discussed previously, sharing your goals with others who can give you help and support is a highly effective way to increase your chances for success.

Without some type of accountability, you are most likely to lose sight of your objectives and you will fail. Therefore, set up a process of reminders to keep you on track. You can use a combination of reminders such as emails, calendars, and reports to keep you organized and focused on your objectives and desired outcomes.

Frequent Review and Re-assessment

When you first sit down and start to define goals it can seem like a difficult and daunting task but over time it begins to get much easier. Patience is required and if you stick to the process, it will become a regular habit for you. Goal Setting is definitely an ongoing process that is never completed; however, each goal will be accomplished over time. Any goals program that defines goals and then ignores them will fail. All goals due in the next year should be reviewed at least once a week and those due in the next month should be reviewed daily. The great thing about frequent review is that this forces you to make big decisions and determine priorities in your life. You should watch for goals that are not being achieved on time or for goals on which you keep extending the deadline.

Overcoming Adversity

Life is full of up and downs. We cannot let it get us frustrated and discouraged. Each of us has faced circumstances that have knocked us down; however, we need to get up and get back into stride. Learn from the experience and move on. We are in control of ourselves.

> *INVICTUS*
> *William Ernest Henley (1849-1903)*
>
> *"Out of the night that covers me,*
> *Black as the Pit from pole to pole,*
> *I thank whatever gods may be*
> *For my unconquerable soul.*
>
> *In the fell clutch of circumstance*
> *I have not winced nor cried aloud.*
> *Under the bludgeoning of chance*
> *My head is bloody, but unbowed.*
>
> *Beyond this place of wrath and tears*
> *Looms but the Horror of the shade,*
> *And yet the menace of the years*
> *Finds, and shall find, me unafraid.*
>
> *It matters not how strait the gate,*
> *How charged with punishments the scroll,*
> *I am the master of my fate,*
> *I am the captain of my soul."*

Another way to look at all that adversity is described in a story that made the rounds via e-mail messages. The question is "When adversity knocks on your door, how do you respond?"

Are you a **CARROT**, an **EGG** or a **COFFEE BEAN**?

> *"A young woman went to her mother and told her about her life and how things were so hard for her. She did not know how she was going to make it and wanted to give up. She was tired of fighting and struggling.*
>
> *It seemed as one problem was solved, a new one arose. Her mother took her to the kitchen. She filled three pots with water and placed each on a high fire. Soon the pots came to boil. In the first, she placed carrots, in the second,*

she placed eggs, and in the last, she placed ground coffee beans. She let them sit and boil, without saying a word.

In about twenty minutes she turned off the burners. She fished the carrots out and placed them in a bowl. She pulled the eggs out and placed them in a bowl. Then she ladled the coffee out and placed it in a bowl.

Turning to her daughter, she asked, "Tell me, what you see?"

"Carrots, eggs, and coffee," she replied. Her mother brought her closer and asked her to feel the carrots. She did and noted that they were soft. The mother then asked the daughter to take an egg and break it. After pulling off the shell, she observed the hard boiled egg. Finally, the mother asked the daughter to sip the coffee. The daughter smiled as she tasted its rich aroma. The daughter then asked, "What does it mean, mother?"

Her mother explained that each of these objects had faced the same adversity ... boiling water. Each reacted differently. The carrot went in strong, hard, and unrelenting.

However, after being subjected to the boiling water, it softened and became weak. The egg had been fragile. Its thin outer shell had protected its liquid interior, but after sitting through the boiling water, its inside became hardened. The ground coffee beans were unique, however. After they were in the boiling water, they had changed the water.

"Which are you?" she asked her daughter.

~~~~~~

Think of this: Which am I? Am I the carrot that seems strong, but with pain and adversity do I wilt and become soft and lose my strength?

Am I the egg that starts with a malleable heart, but

changes with the heat? Did I have a fluid spirit, but after a death, a breakup, a financial hardship or some other trial, have I become hardened and stiff? Does my shell look the same, but on the inside am I bitter and tough with a stiff spirit and hardened heart?

Or am I like the coffee bean? The bean actually changes the hot water, the very circumstance that brings the pain. When the water gets hot, it releases the fragrance and flavor. If you are like the bean, when things are at their worst, you get better and change the situation around you. When the hour is the darkest and trials are their greatest, do you elevate yourself to another level? How do you handle adversity?

"ARE YOU A **CARROT**, AN **EGG**, OR A **COFFEE BEAN**?"

~~~~~~

May you have enough happiness to make you sweet, enough trials to make you strong, enough sorrow to keep you human and enough hope to make you happy.

The happiest of people don't necessarily have the best of everything; they just make the most of everything that comes along their way.

The brightest future will always be based on a forgotten past; you can't go forward in life until you let go of your past failures and heartaches.

When you were born, you were crying and everyone around you was smiling.

Live your life so at the end, you're the one who is smiling and everyone around you is crying."

INTEGRATION (BRINGING IT ALL TOGETHER)

Everything we have learned has to be brought together and integrated into a cohesive whole. Our actions need to be continuous and linked from step to step with the ability to jump around as needed. It is no longer linear but rather an integrated system with many loops. Integration gives you the ability to bring together the diverse logical and imagination sources from both within and outside your mind into a single coherent framework.

Questioning & Learning

How can you improve your ability to learn from your mistakes and experiences? How can you develop your independence of thought?
How do you maintain an insatiable quest for knowledge and continuous improvement?
Are you asking the right questions?

You must question things around you. Be an independent thinker. Demonstrate things for yourself. Leonardo da Vinci is considered to be one of the world's few multi-talented geniuses. He would look at a problem from many different perspectives. People like him are literally able to place themselves completely in someone else's shoes in order to experience a new way of looking at things. This approach expands their knowledge and consciousness of the world around them.

Leonardo da Vinci believed that, to gain knowledge about the form of a problem, you must begin by learning how to restructure it in many different ways. He believed that the first way you look at a problem is entirely too biased. You are only seeing the problem from one perspective - yours.

To expand your awareness, you must consistently seek opportunities for growth. Look for new relationships, expand your knowledge, and step out of your comfort zone.

Are you balancing Art & Science, and Logic & Imagination both at home and work? Most people are stuck in either the left or right brain mode. One of the most significant characteristics of highly creative people is their openness to the unknown and willingness to use their intuition. Gelb stated in his book on da Vinci "As a leading thinker, da Vinci learned to translate imagination into a technical language…Major breakthroughs are experienced through intuition." Let your mind go free and generate thoughts on whatever comes to your mind. Later, you can look for connections and organize those thoughts.

Managing Ambiguity and Change
The amount, magnitude, pace, and complexity of change continues to accelerate but, do not let it overwhelm you. If something is very important to us and the outcome is uncertain, it creates a level of anxiety. The ability to manage ambiguity and change is a learned life skill. If you manage change effectively, it can be exciting and create a creative tension that can lead to opportunity.

You need to be positive, and have the self-confidence to succeed. Having developed a clear vision of what you want to achieve will help you to anticipate what is coming and provides a sense of control. As part of the planning process, you would have gone through some "what if" scenarios and prepared for the possibility of change so that you will rarely be surprised.

By accepting change as a part of life, you can look for opportunities in changing situations. You work with your personal strengths and avoid your weaknesses. Being proactive enables you to work the change in a positive way rather than spending your time and efforts defending against it.

Systems' Thinking
How do all the pieces that were discussed fit together? Do you recognize and appreciate how interconnected things are to each other? Systems' thinking is an approach for developing models to promote our understanding of events, patterns of behavior resulting in the events, and even more importantly, the underlying structure responsible for the patterns of behavior. If

we are interested in addressing a particular situation, it is only through our understanding of the underlying structure that we will be able to identify the most appropriate leverage points to effect change within the system.

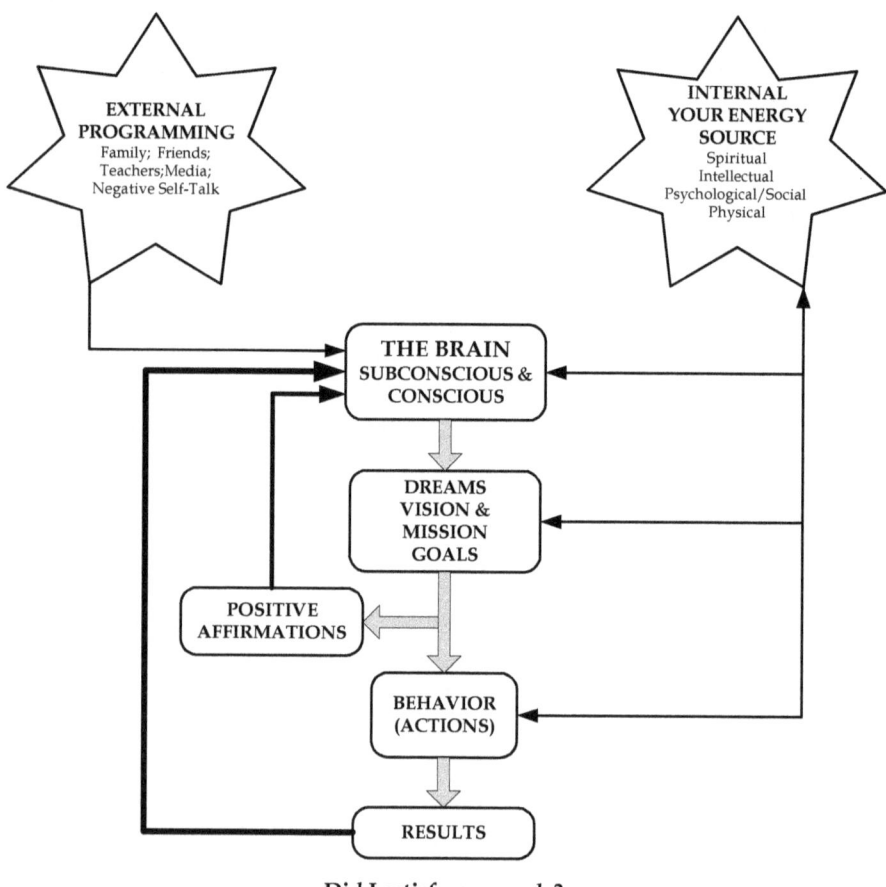

Did I satisfy my needs?

Systems' thinking is your ability to relate things as a whole (or holistically) including the many different types of relationships between the many elements in a complex system. Systems' thinking is an approach that focuses on the whole, not the parts, of a complex system. It concentrates on the interfaces and boundaries of components, on their connections and arrangement, on the potential for holistic systems to achieve *results that are greater than the sum of the parts*. Systems' thinking is a framework for seeing interrelationships rather than things, for seeing both the forest *and* the trees. As such, systems' thinking is one of those related disciplines that enhances quality efforts. Applied in partnership with quality activities, systems thinking serves as a lens to see beyond self-limiting perspectives.

ACTION ITEM 18: Visualize your goals. Draw a representation of them – create a mind map!!!

> Step 1 – Sketch your big picture. Create your own personal logo. Take time to allow the image to form in your head and allow it to emerge. On lines radiating out from your logo, brainstorm items representing the key areas of your life, such as, career, family, spirituality, etc. Try to capture what it is that you want in each of these areas.
>
> Step 2 – Explore your mission and vision. Answer the question "What do you want?" Redraw your brainstorming mind map into something more organized, using multi-colors to help you to bring it all into something that is visually alive. Explore each branch in depth.
>
> Step 3 – Clarify your core values. Answer the question "Why do you want it?" and "Why is it important?"
>
> Step 4 – Contemplate your purpose. Answer the questions "What is your purpose?" And "What your purpose is not?"
>
> Step 5 – Assess current reality. Review the major areas of your life assessing the status as objectively as possible.
>
> Step 6 – Look for connections. Are there any key ideas or words that re-appear in the mind map? Is your life in proportion? Are the connections and proportions in line? Where are the greatest

gaps between what you want and where you are? Are you on course to realizing your most important goals? What adjustments do you need to make to keep everything in balance?

Step 7 – Strategize for change. You defined your vision and mission by contemplating "What do I want?" You clarified your values and purpose by contemplating "Why do I want it?" Now design a strategy by answering, "How will I get it?"

Success Comes to Those Who Work the Process

In his book, Laws of Success, page 64, Napoleon Hill, while discussing Thomas Alva Edison, states:

> "Yes, he succeeded – but- he almost failed!" So did Robert Fulton [inventor of the steamboat] and Abraham Lincoln and nearly all the others whom we call successful. No man ever achieved worth-while success who did not, at one time or other, find himself with at least one foot hanging well over the brink of failure."

In his book "More Than Money", Neil Cavuto writes about successful people who did not give up when things were not going very well. On page ix, he states:

> "To me, greatness is defined not by how we handle all that goes well for us, but how we deal with all that does not."

He provides insights to people who had to face real tragedies in their life and how they chose to fight those situations. On page xiii - xiv, he states

> *"The lucky ones are the people who make their suffering and losses the sources of new powerful, enduring motivation."*

You have established clarity of your guiding principles. When you know what is important to you, you can develop your strategy to accomplish your goals. If you believe in your capabilities and have a passion or a driving force pushing you along, you will achieve. As discussed, in order to make it all work for you, the fundamental principles to follow are:

- The plan MUST be written
- Avoid too much detail
- The plan should be feasible
- Review and modify periodically (at least once every few months).

> *"Knowing is not enough; we must apply.*
> *Willing is not enough; we must do."* –
> **Johann Wolfgang von Goethe**

ACTION ITEM 19: Be sure you are living and working your plan. As previously discussed, this must be a documented effort utilizing a notebook, a paper day planner, or a computerized device. Make periodic checks of your plan. Set up your calendar for the next six months with specific dates to review your values, mission, vision, and goals. In developing your plan, you documented your values, your mission, and vision. After you have lived with them for a while, you should conduct a review and make whatever adjustments needed to move forward with your goals.

If you made the paradigm shift we talked about, you will have started down your path to achieve success. It is important for you to create a continuous review and follow-up process to keep it all working for you. The steps in our system will set up the path but you must work at following it.

"Give me six hours to chop down a tree and I will spend the first four sharpening the axe." -
Abraham Lincoln

Step 7

SELF-RENEWAL (RECHARGE YOUR ENERGY SOURCE)

> *"And in the end, it's not the years in your life that count. It's the life in your years."* — Abraham Lincoln

A person must use all facets of their being to be a balanced person. Too much focus on one area of their life, such as the job, will eventually do harm to their overall well-being. One must learn to strike a balance among all parts of their life. For many of us, as we work, we become focused on the work at hand. We can become so involved in what it is we are striving for, that we lose sight of the total picture.

When we become so involved, we can begin to lose perspective. Our perspective becomes solely that of achieving the one item in front of us and as the pressure builds up, it will begin to wear us down. The consequence of this wearing down is a loss of enthusiasm and lack of passion to achieve our goals.

> *"We may run, walk, stumble, drive, or fly, but let us never lose sight of the reason for the journey, or miss a chance to see a rainbow on the way."* - **Gloria Gaither**

Just as batteries need to be recharged after they have been used for a period, so do humans. After periods of intense work, sleep alone is not enough to prevent the human body from burning out. People loose energy and we need to recharge both our mind and body.

It has been shown that people do better when they take a break from the routine and take some time for themselves. This break provides us with a chance to relax both our mind and body. We might indulge in an activity that is more demanding physically or mentally but it will be a change in our routine. This change provides us with the diversion that we need.

Most people get their best ideas when they are relaxed and by themselves, resting their total being. For some of us it comes while we are in bed, for others it comes when we are enjoying nature, and for still others it comes from enjoying a "diversion" such as music or art. Virtually no one claims it happens while they are at work. These creative breakthroughs come about when a person's mind and body is relaxed and free from stress.

When things in your life seem almost too much to handle, when 24 hours in a day are not enough, think of the following story that made the rounds on the e-mail circuit.

A professor stood before his Philosophy 101 class and had some items in front of him. When the class began, wordlessly, he picked up a very large and empty mayonnaise jar and proceeded to fill it with golf balls.

He then asked the students if the jar was full.

They agreed that it was.

So the professor then picked up a box of pebbles and poured them into the jar. He shook the jar lightly. The pebbles rolled into the open areas between the golf balls. He then asked the students again if the jar was full.

They agreed it was.

The professor next picked up a box of sand and poured it into the jar. Of course, the sand filled up everything else. He asked once more if the jar was full.

The students responded with a unanimous "yes."

The professor then produced two cans of beer from under the table and poured the entire contents into the jar, effectively filling the empty space between the sand. The students laughed.

"Now," said the professor, as the laughter subsided, "I want you to recognize that this jar represents your life. The golf balls are the important things--your family, your children, your health, your friends, your favorite passions--things that if everything else was lost and only they remained, your life would still be full. "The pebbles are the other things that matter like your job, your house, your car. The sand is everything else--the small stuff.

If you put the sand into the jar first," he continued, "there is no room for the pebbles or the golf balls. The same goes for life. If you spend all your time and energy on the small stuff, you will never have room for the things

> *that are important to you.*
>
> *Pay attention to the things that are critical to your happiness. Play with your children. Take time to get medical checkups. Take your partner out to dinner. Play another 18.*
>
> *There will always be time to clean the house, and mow the lawn. "Take care of the golf balls first, the things that really matter. Set your priorities. The rest is just sand."*
>
> *One of the students raised her hand and inquired what the beer represented.*
>
> *The professor smiled. "I'm glad you asked. It just goes to show you that no matter how full your life may seem, there's always room for a couple of beers."*

The golf balls represent that which is most important to you. If you did not put the golf balls in first, you would not have been able to put them in later. The other major point to the story is to make the time to relax. One of the key elements of achieving is your ability to keep your life in balance. You must take the time to take care of yourself in the key areas of personal development. These are definitely Quadrant 2 activities (see page 169). You should ask yourself:

- What should I be doing more of?
- What should I be doing less of?
- What should I start doing to improve the quality of my life?
- What should I stop doing to create the time to do the things that are most important to me?

Focus on the long term but take care of the short-term needs. Renew yourself so that you can have the energy to get where you want to be. The four key areas to work on are: 1) Spiritual, 2) Intellectual, 3)Psychological/Social, and 4) Physical. Let us address each one.

SPIRITUAL

Spirituality may mean something different to each one of us and some people use the term interchangeably with religion. Whether you are religious or not, most people recognize the existence of a Divine Power and the need to have help from the spiritual higher power, or at least of something greater than oneself. Regardless of how you define it, spirituality can be a source of inner peace, purpose, and support. We need to eliminate all barriers to spiritual activities. This recognition and the effort to exist within the harmony will keep your core in alignment. It enables you to connect with your inner self, your guiding principles, and your mission. This can come from religious scripture, great literature, meditation, and / or nature study.

Religious input is a way to nourish your being. For many, the belief in an all-powerful God provides both a rationale for all that occurs in the universe and a guiding light as to values, guiding principles, and life behaviors. You are of His design and He will help you to achieve the maximum performance you are capable of achieving.

Meditation is one form of clearing your mind of spurious activity and calm yourself to hear and feel what is happening around you. It is a state of concentrated attention on some object of thought or awareness and results in a state of relaxation. In a very basic form, you can sit quietly with your legs crossed and breathe slowly and deeply. Keep your eyes closed and silently repeat the phrase "I am." Meditating helps you to find and tap into the source of your inner strength, energy, and peace. The meditative state results in an overall quieting of the brain and it becomes more receptive to inputs. Different meditative techniques encompass a wide range of spiritual and/or physical practices.

Another approach can be the study and practice of Yoga, which is a discipline that promotes spiritual unity with a supreme being through a system of postures and rituals and invokes meditation as one part of the practice. The word Yoga comes from Sanskrit and it means to yoke or bring together the mind, body, and spirit.

Spirituality is very important in our lives as it can improve the quality of your life in the following ways:

- Reduce anxiety and stress
- Encourage feelings of hope and empowerment
- Stimulate self-awareness and personal growth
- Develop a positive mental attitude
- Assist in discovering a life purpose
- Create an inner peace

ACTION ITEM 20: Make sure you make time for some form of spiritual alignment. Find a place to practice your spirituality. You may choose a church, temple, or other place of worship or a quiet room in your home. Schedule time for prayer, meditation, relaxation techniques, or whatever gives you inner peace. Learn what you believe in and why you do, then follow your beliefs.

INTELLECTUAL

Develop your brain and do not be a couch potato. If you are going to watch TV, in addition to your "chill-out" show(s) to entertain you, choose some shows that inform or inspire you, as well. Intellectual wellness involves life-long learning. Thinking, memory, learning, reading, writing, and communications are part of intellectual wellness.

Take time to read. Reading exposes you to new ideas that you can use both in your professional and personal lives. As you process the new ideas, you will also be exercising your logic and understanding abilities. Try reading biographies of people you admire to learn more about their lives.

Do you continually position yourself to learn? Think about skills you need to perform in your everyday life but are weak at performing. Work at improving that skill. Learn what you must to improve and practice until you have achieved competency in that skill.

In his book, "Change Your Brain, Change Your Body" Dr. Amen discusses the link between a "healthy" brain and your body. He has a medical practice that works on boosting your brain to improve weight control, heart functions, energy levels and ability to focus. He talks about the brain as being "the command and control center of your body." I mention his book and approach because here is another reinforcement of using your brain to control your body, both physically and emotionally. Dr. Amen wants everyone to work on renewing themselves by being both physically and mentally fit.

Think about other ways you can exercise your mind as well as your body. Internal peace comes from living a life that is balanced and in harmony with your guiding principles.

ACTION ITEM 21: Make sure you schedule time to read one educational book each month or more often, if possible.

PSYCHOLOGICAL/SOCIAL

Get involved in an interest group, team sport, or church group. Meet people and choose those with whom you seem to get along with or whom you believe can provide you with social stimulation. Winners know other winners. As you get to know people, get yourself introduced to their friends who most likely have much in common with you.

Work on providing service and contributing to others. Provide some outlets and social interaction.

ACTION ITEM 22: Make time to regularly initiate a phone call or visit with family, relatives, and friends.

PHYSICAL

Good health is our greatest asset and maintaining it should be a priority. If you do not already have a fitness routine, go through the following questions:

- Have you had a health check lately?
- Do you exercise regularly?
- Are you making time to keep yourself physically fit?
- Do you eat well?
- What are your sleep habits? Are you getting enough sleep?
- Are you drinking enough water (2-3 quarts per day)?

You need to take care of yourself physically as the health of your body will influence your well-being and determine how much energy you have. Therefore, you will need to make time for some sort of physical exercise. It can be of any type of competitive sport or exercise program. The important thing is that it be regular and consistent.

If you have not been exercising regularly, it is important to schedule a visit with your doctor for a check-up. Elicit advice from your doctor about what you are capable of doing. Begin slowly, doing a realistic exercise routine for your condition. Exercise a few times a week and get yourself into a regular routine. You would want to build your strength, endurance, and flexibility to ensure you are most effective in all your endeavors.

In addition to physical exercise, the other side of the health coin is to be sure you eat a well-balanced diet. You can be a meat and potatoes person, a vegetarian, or anything in between. You need to be sure you are eating properly, including a variety of proteins, carbohydrates, and vegetables. Enjoying a balanced diet will keep you healthy and strong and provide the physical force you will need to keep you energized.

ACTION ITEM 23: If you have not had a health check, schedule it as soon as reasonably possible. Exercise regularly by walking, running, swimming, or working out. Begin a regimen of both aerobic exercise and strength training. Introduce some sports time, such as playing tennis, golf, etc.

Also, you must be careful and ensure you are getting the proper nutrition. Try to avoid highly processed foods. Improve the quality of the foods you eat. Limit your red meat and dairy products while increasing your input of whole foods such as beans, grains, vegetables, fruits, and fish.

"The people who get on in this world are the people who get up and look for the circumstances they want and if they can't find them, make them." -
George Bernard Shaw

EPILOGUE – FIT FOR LIFE

> *"The greatest danger for most of us is not that our aim is too high and we miss it, but that it is too low and we reach it."* — Michelangelo

Throughout this book, you examined your habits, both good and bad, and began to change those that you felt needed to be changed. You decided on a course of action which, with self-discipline and initiatives, will change your life. You will need commitment and lots of follow through to accomplish the programs and achieve your goals. There will be times when you will have to force yourself to follow through and take the correct actions, however the more you do it, the easier it becomes. These actions will cause you to break old "bad" habits and form new "good" habits that will work for you the rest of your life.

Remember, if you expect to change your life, you must aim high. Yes, you may need a bit of reality, but you still must reach beyond what you believe are your current abilities and stretch yourself. You will develop the habits that will keep you fit for the rest of your life. Too many of us lose sight of what is good for us. We become lazy and lethargic. We look at short-term gain rather than what is happening to us over the long term. These key areas of self-transformation will enable us to become highly disciplined and focused people.

Everyone experiences bad situations or down days. We must

prepare ourselves for all kinds of situations and learn to "go with the flow." Think about trees in a storm. The trees that survive the storm bend and flex, while those that are too rigid, crack and break.

A specific example is the evergreen tree in a snowstorm. The branches, when covered with heavy, wet snow, bend under the load. With the melting snow, the branches spring back and continue to grow. Occasionally, a branch breaks in the wind or under a snow load, but the tree recovers and grows on. As with the trees, we must not allow a situation to break us. We must get past the situation, learn from the experience and grow stronger.

Aim for the heavens and reach for a star. Dream the impossible dream; stretch your desires no matter how far out there they are. Even if you fall short of the star, you will be somewhere in the heavens, way beyond where you are now.

If you have been performing the activities along your journey, you have been travelling the *Road to Master Your Personal and Professional Life*. Have a good journey and

BECOME A WINNER
&
LIVE LIFE YOUR WAY!

GLOSSARY

Affirmation: a positive reinforcement.

Ethics: a set of moral principles; the principles of conduct governing an individual or a group; a guiding philosophy.

Effectiveness: - a measure of the positive results that are obtained to accomplish a purpose no matter what the cost.

Efficacy: - the capacity to produce the desired result or effect both efficiently and effectively.

Efficient: - degree to which objectives are achieved with the least amount of effort, time, and resources.

Goal: - is the long-range, well-defined target or end toward which effort is directed.

Guiding Principle(s): - a deeply held driving force, a rule of action or conduct, a foundation for our actions, a core belief, and highest priority; they define boundaries and govern our mode of conduct; a high truth and that for which we will take a stand.

Holistic or Whole picture overview: — the recognition of patterns of light, sound or thought.

Mission: - deals with the present and describes your fundamental purpose and plan of how to achieve your vision. It is the process to follow to get to your destination.

Paradigm: a philosophical or theoretical framework of any kind; a basic set of assumptions.

Paradigm Shift: a revolutionary, transformation, or drastic change in your belief system.

Positive Sensory Visualization: - is a technique where you guide your brain to create a total mental image of the outcome you want to achieve. Your visualization includes not only truly seeing the achievement of your dream but all the facets around it, including hear, touch, taste, and smell.

Principle(s): - is a rule or code of conduct; a comprehensive and fundamental law, doctrine, or assumption, a truth that is the foundation for other truths; a basic truth, comprehensive and fundamental law, doctrine, or assumption: the principles of democracy; a rule, code of conduct, or standard, especially of good behavior: a man of principle; the collectivity of moral or ethical standards or judgments; a fixed or predetermined policy or mode of action; a basic or essential quality or element determining intrinsic nature or characteristic behavior: the principle of self-preservation.

Qualities: - character or nature, as belonging to or distinguishing a thing: *the quality of a sound*; character with respect to fineness, or grade of excellence: *food of poor quality; silks of fine quality*; high grade; superiority; excellence: *wood grain of quality*; a personality or character trait: *kindness is one of her many good qualities*.

Spatial awareness: — the ability to imagine, and operate within, three-dimensional space.

Systems: — a set of organized interacting components creating an interactive whole. Although it can encompass very complex mathematical models, it is used here to indicate an organized approach based on experience.

Values: - A principle, standard, or quality considered worthwhile or desirable; to place importance upon something; beliefs of a person or social group in which they have an emotional investment (either for or against something); is something intrinsically valuable or desirable and our values act as our compass, guiding us through life's terrain, however, values are developed and can change as we experience life. As defined by the World Book Dictionary, "it is an established ideal of life, objects, customs, ways of acting, and the like, that the members of a given society regards as desirable." They are the reasons to set goals and motives to take the journey towards achieving those goals. Values are similar to but differ from both Ethics and Guiding Principles.

Virtues: - moral excellence; goodness; righteousness; conformity of one's life and conduct to moral and ethical principles; uprightness; rectitude; a particular moral excellence; a good or admirable quality or property.

Vision: - deals with the future and describes what, where, and who you want to become. It is an ideal that provides the framework to focus your energies and efforts which will guide your choices.

BIBLIOGRAPHY

Amen, M.D., Daniel G. <u>Change Your Brain, Change Your Body</u>, New York, Harmony Books, 2010, 613AME

Begley, Sharon. <u>Train Your Mind Change Your Brain</u>, New York, Ballantine Books, 2007, 153BEG

Benson, M.D., Herbert. <u>The Relaxation Response</u>, New York, Morrow, 1975, 616.132BEN

Benson, M.D., Herbert, William Proctor. <u>The Break-Out Principle</u>, New York, Scribner, 2003, 158.1BEN

Bolles, Richard Nelson. <u>What Color Is Your Parachute?</u>, New York, Ten Speed Press, 2008, 331.128BOL

Buzon, Tony. <u>The Mind Map Book</u>, New York, Penguin Books, 1994, 153.4BUZ

Cavuto, Neil. <u>More Than Money</u>, New York, HarperCollins Publishers Inc., 2004, 170.44CAV

Covey, Stephen R. <u>The Seven Habits of Highly Effective People</u>, New York, Simon & Schuster 1989

Covey, Stephen R., A. Roger Merrill, and Rebecca R. Merrill, <u>First Things First</u>, New York, Simon & Schuster 1994, 158.1COV

Doidge, Norman, M.D. <u>The Brain That Changes Itself</u>, New York, Penguin Group, 2007, 612.8DOI

Frankl, Viktor. <u>Man's Search for Meaning Revised and Enlarged Third Edition</u>, Simon & Schuster, 1984, 150.1957FRA

Franklin, Benjamin. <u>The Autobiography of Benjamin Franklin</u>, Roslyn, NY, Walter J. Black, Inc. 1941, 128-140

Gardner, Howard, <u>Leading Minds</u>, New York, Basic Books, 1995

Gelb, Michael J. <u>How to Think like Leonardo da Vinci</u>, Delacorte Press, 1998, 153.35 Leo Gel

Germer, Christopher K. the mindful path to self-compassion, New York, The Guilford Press, 2009, 152.4GER

Graham, Stedman. <u>You Can Make It Happen</u>, Simon & Schuster, 1997, 650.1GRA

Green, Thad, <u>motivation management</u>, California, Davies-Black Publishing, 2000, 658.314GRE

Giuliani, Rudolph W., <u>Leadership</u>, New York, Hyperion, 2002

Hansen, Mark Victor, and Linkletter, Art. <u>How to Make the Rest of Your Life the Best of Your Life</u>, Nelson Books, 2006

Harary, PhD, Keith, and Donahue, PhD, Eileen. <u>Who Do You Think You Are?</u>, New York, HarperSanFrancisco, HarperCollinsPublishers, 1994, 155.283HAR

Hill, Napoleon. <u>Think and Grow Rich</u>, Hawthorn Books, Inc. 1967, 158.1HIL see p363

----.   <u>The Master-Key to Riches</u>, Hawthorn Books, Inc. 1968, 158.1HIL

----. The Law of Success in Sixteen Lessons 3rd Edition, Chicago, IL, Success Unlimited Inc. 1969, 650.1HIL

----. Keys to Success, Plume. 1997

Hobbs, Charles R. Time Power, Charles R. Hobbs Corporation, Audio Cassettes, 1983

Huntsman, Jon M. Winners never Cheat, Upper Saddle River, NJ, Wharton School Publishing, 2005, 174 HUN

Jason, Kathryn, and Joe McMahon, PhD, The Power to Change Your Life, New York, NY, Doubleday & Co, 1982, 158.1JAS

Keirsey, David, Please Understand Me II: Temperament Character Intelligence, Del Mar, CA, Prometheus Nemesis, 1998, 155.26KEI

Kise, Jane A.G., David Stark, and Sandra Krebs Hirsh, Life Keys, Minneapolis, MN, Bethany Press International, 1996, 158.1KIS

Kroeger, Otto, with Thuesen, Janet M. Type Talk at Work, New York, Delacorte Press, 1992, 155.264KRO

Lore, Nicholas. The Pathfinder, New York, Fireside, 1998

Lowe, Tamara. Get Motivated, New York, Doubleday, 2009, 153.8DWO

Mackenzie, R. Alec. The Time Trap: Third Edition, New York, AMACOM, 1997

Maltz, Maxwell. Psycho-Cybernetics, New York, Simon & Schuster, 1960 158.1MAL

----. The Search for Self-Respect, New York, Grosset & Dunlap, 1973 170.202MAL

Marsh, Henry. The Breakthrough Factor, New York, Simon & Schuster 1997 158.1MAR

Maslow, Abraham H. Maslow on Management, John Wiley & Sons, 1998 158.7MAS

----. Toward a Psychology of Being, Third Edition, John Wiley & Sons, 1999 155.25MAS

McCay, James T. The Management of Time, Englewood Cliffs, NJ, Prentice-Hall, 1959 158.7MCC

Norris, Chuck. The Secret Power Within, New York, Little, Brown, & Company, 1996, 796.8NOR

Peck, M. Scott. The Road Less Traveled, Simon & Schuster, 1978

Robbins, Anthony. Unlimited Power, New York, Simon & Schuster, 1986 158.1ROB

----. Awaken the Giant Within, New York, Simon & Schuster, 1991 158.1ROB

Rokeach, Milton. Beliefs, Attitudes, and Values, Jossey-Bass, Inc, Publishers, 1968

----. The Nature of Human Values, The Free Press, 1973

Sedlar, Jeri, & Rick Miners. Don't Retire, REWIRE! 2nd Edition, Alpha Books, Penguin Books, NY 2007 650.14SED

Sher, Barbara. I Could Do Anything if I only knew what it was, Delacorte Press, 1994

Sommer, Bobbe, and Maxwell Maltz Foundation, Psycho-Cybernetics 2000, Paramus, NJ, Prentice Hall, 1993

Souza, Brian. Become Who You Were Born to Be, Harmony Books, New York, 2005, 158.1SOU

Tieger, Paul D. & Barbara Barron-Tieger, Do What You Are, Little, Brown and Company, 2001

Tracy, Brian. Time Power, New York, AMACOM, 2004, 650.11TRA

Viscott, David. The Viscott Method, Boston, Houghton Mifflin, 1984

Waitley, Denis. The Psychology of Winning, Chicago, IL, Nightingale-Conant Corporation, 1979

Good News Bible, New York, American Bible Society, 1978

INDEX

A

Action Item 44, 69, 101, 109, 119, 121, 130, 134, 139, 143, 156, 159, 166, 171, 173, 179, 184, 195, 197, 204, 205, 206, 207
Affirmation 119, 122
Aristotle 117
Aurelius, Marcus 117

B

Bell, Dr. Gerald 56
Berkeley Personality Profile. 63, 66, 89
Berlin, Isaiah 52
Berra, Yogi 171
Brain 50, 205
    left brain 27, 50
    right brain 27, 193
Buddha 183
Buzan, Tony 140

C

Carroll, Lewis 49, 147
Cavuto, Neil 196
Choices 39
Commitment 184, 186
Confucius 155, 163
Control 40
Coolidge, Calvin 184
Covey, Stephen 125, 169
CREATE 136

D

da Vinci, Leonardo 125, 192
Decision making 177
Desiderata 144
Desires 36, 37

E

Edison, Thomas Alva 116
Efficacy 170
Einstein, Albert 127
Esteem 38, 54, 74
Ethics 95

F

Failure 113, 115
Frankl, Victor 41, 42, 132
Franklin, Ben 57, 97, 101

G

Goal .. 28, 148, 150, 156, 174, 179
    Goals Table 159
    SMART Goals 150
Green, Thad 37
Guiding Principles 27, 44, 91, 94, 95, 145, 147, 172

H

Habit 184, 186, 187
Henley, William Ernest 189
Hill, Napoleon 126, 181, 196
Hobbs, Charles R. 169
Hugo, Victor 185

I

Integration 192
Invictus 189

J

Johari Window 64

K

Keller, Helen 182
Kettering, Charles F. 111
King, Martin Luther 38, 172

L

Lao-Tzu 47
Life Management 28
Linkletter, Art 183
Lombardi, Vince 185
Lowe, Tamara 37

M

Major Definite Purpose 126
Maltz, Dr. Maxwell iv, 113, 114, 151
Maslow, Abraham 35, 53, 54, 55, 73, 152
McKay, James 175, 176
Michelangelo 209
Mind Map 10, 140, 141, 195
Mission ... 28, 125, 126, 132, 145, 147, 173, 174
    Personal Mission Statement
    .... 132, 137
Motivation 36, 37, 184, 186
Myers-Briggs 59, 65, 66, 87
    Extraversion vs.
    Introversion 60
    Perceiving vs. Judging 61
    Sensing vs. Intuition 60
    Thinking vs. Feeling 60

N

Needs hierarchy ... 35, 53, 54, 55, 73, 74, 152
    Esteem Needs 54
    Physiological Needs 54
    Safety/Security Needs 54
    Self-Actualization 55, 74
    Social/Belonging Needs ... 54
Needs, wants, and desires 35, 36, 37, 54, 55, 66, 73, 74, 82, 152

P

paradigm 21
Patanjali i
pattern 33, 34, 50, 51, 66, 69, 138
Perseverance 29
Personal Inventory 56, 71
Personal Vision 127
Personality Types 58, 59
Plan 155, 163, 164, 169
Plato 49
Positive Sensory Visualization
.... 117
Principles 33, 95
Procrastination 174
Psycho-Cybernetics . iv, 28, 113, 114

Q

Quadrant 2 170
Qualities 94, 95

R

Reality Model 55
Rogers, Will 175
Roles 138

S

SCARED 39, 40
Schedule 69, 169, 184, 204
self-assessment ii
Self-Assured 28
Self-Awareness 27
Self-Confidence.................... 116
Self-Directed Search 61, 88
Self-Renewal 29
Shakespeare, William 93
SMART Goals
    Attainable.......................... 151
    Measurable 151
    Relevant............................ 152
    Specific 150
    Time-specific.................... 152
Spiritual 57, 78, 153, 159
Star Wars 21
Stevenson, Robert Louis........ 19
Strong Interest Inventory 61
subconscious ...iv, 21, 22, 25, 36, 38, 41, 43, 45, 112, 113, 116, 118, 119, 120, 121, 136, 164
Success23, 71, 113, 114, 117, 196
Systems 193, 194

T

Teams 179
    Support Team 28
Time Management............... 168
TO-DO 164
Transform ii
Twain, Mark 146

V

Values 33, 94, 95
Verne, Jules 22
Virtues 94, 95
Viscott, David .... vi, 44
Vision 28, 125, 128, 132, 138, 145, 147, 174
von Goethe, Johann Wolfgang
    .... 42, 197

W

Wants 35, 36
Winner .... vi, 41, 43, 185, 206
Wintle, Walter D. 117
WOTS Up 30, 67, 90, 91
    Opportunities..................... 68
    Strengths 68
    Threats/Constraints 68
    Weaknesses 67

ORDER FORM

For additional copies of this book (Eyes On Winning Ways), please send check or money order to:

Eyes On Communications LLC
120 E. Main St, Suite 317
Ramsey, NJ 07446
OR go to www.eyesoncommunications.com

Book	$19.95
New Jersey Residents add 7% State sales tax $1.40	
S & H in the continental US	$3.50
TOTAL	

PLEASE PRINT
Name:_____

Address:_____

City:_____ State:_____ Zip:_____

Email:_____

Autograph to:

_____

_____

PAYMENT:
Check   Money Order

www.ingramcontent.com/pod-product-compliance
Lightning Source LLC
Chambersburg PA
CBHW061257110426
42742CB00012BA/1954